"This is a book for those wh[...] ; about the way we are doing our [...] get on the consumer track and 'do truth,' th[...] this book will help you reverse the trend and go in a direction that is more satisfying to the soul because it gets to the heart of what worship is all about."

Robert E. Webber, Myers Professor of Ministry, Northern Seminary

"Here's a book on worship to be read by every church musician, pastor, leader, and worshiper."

Leith Anderson, author, *Jesus: An Intimate Portrait of the Man, His Land, and His People*

"The desire to worship is rooted in our hunger for heaven. Our coming together for worship is a foretaste of heaven. In his book that is both spiritual and intensely practical at the same time, Kevin Navarro explores this vital connection between our fragmented experience in the here and now and the hope we all share for the time that certainly will come when heaven will come for us."

Michael Card, award-winning musician; author, *A Sacred Sorrow*

"Weekly worship can be much more than a dreary duty; as Navarro ably demonstrates, the complete worship service can be the appetizer course at your church for the heavenly banquet to come. Navarro writes with the heart of a worshiper, a pastor, and a jazz musician. *The Complete Worship Service* is filled with biblical insight and practical application. Pastors and lay leaders alike will benefit from Navarro's field-tested recommendations for practicing welcoming hospitality and designing meaningful worship services. I can't think of a better book to stimulate and inform conversations in your church about worship that engages the whole people and the whole person."

Robb Redman, author, *The Great Worship Awakening*

"When it comes to worship, nothing matters if the only one worthy of worship is just a footnote beneath worship glitz. Kevin Navarro prods our hearts back to Jesus and to worship services that give life, not just lessons; a foretaste of heaven, not just so many factoids to get through another week. *The Complete Worship Service* is a timely, passionate antidote to the worship humanism saturating contemporary services."

Sally Morgenthaler, author, *Worship Evangelism*; founder,
Sacramentis.com

"Here is a book that anyone dissatisfied with the quality, Christ- and Scripture-centered nature, or impact of their worship services must read. While some may feel that Navarro's goals of excellence at times lie beyond their reach, no one can doubt his heart for seeing people brought to Christ and brought up in him through worship. Navarro's track record, moreover, first as a worship pastor and then as a senior pastor at a church where I once served as an interim, speaks for itself—steady (not spectacular) growth, qualitatively and quantitatively, in a congregation that dearly loves this infectiously upbeat leader who also models integrity and humility in everything he does."

Craig L. Blomberg, Distinguished Professor of New Testament,
Denver Seminary

"When I closed this book, I felt a tremendous mixture of hope, excitement, affirmation, and renewed devotion to the work of crafting weekly worship services. Kevin Navarro ennobles the entire effort of preparing the Sunday 'dress rehearsals' for our ultimate worship experience in heaven. I'm grateful for the hard-won lessons, practical advice, and inspiring vision offered in these pages. Let our weekly celebrations resound with greater joy, profound hope, and a taste of eternity whenever we gather together!"

Nancy Beach, teaching pastor and creative director,
Willow Creek Community Church

—— *The* ——

COMPLETE
WORSHIP
SERVICE

The COMPLETE WORSHIP SERVICE

Creating a Taste of Heaven on Earth

KEVIN J. NAVARRO

BakerBooks

Grand Rapids, Michigan

Published by Baker Books
a division of Baker Publishing Group
P.O. Box 6287, Grand Rapids, MI 49516-6287
www.bakerbooks.com

Printed in the United States of America

Library of Congress Cataloging-in-Publication Data
Navarro, Kevin J.
    The complete worship service : creating a taste of heaven on earth / Kevin J. Navarro.
        p.   cm.
    Includes bibliographical references.
    ISBN 0-8010-9183-7 (pbk.)
    1. Worship. I. Title.
    BV10.3.N38 2005
    264—dc22   2005009081

CONTENTS

FOREWORD

As I sat down to read *The Complete Worship Service*, my mind wandered back to 1970 and to the beginnings of the worship phenomenon. Since I am now on the older side of life, I am able to remember the time when worship was completely disregarded by the evangelical community.

That's right! Disregarded. Worship was the last issue people talked about. Everyone discussed evangelism, missions, and education, and there was even a little talk about social justice. But worship? Why would anyone talk about worship?

And then came the explosion. First in the Catholic Church with the Liturgical Constitution published in 1963. Then the renewal in the mainline churches. And finally an earthquake hit the evangelical church—contemporary choruses, the renaissance of the arts, the seeker church, church growth principles, worship conferences, worship fests, workshops on worship, worship 24/7 on TV, worship concerts, worship magazines, worship education. A whole new industry was birthed around worship. Buy this book, this CD, this lecture. Do this, do that, go here, go there. It is consumerism gone mad. So the pendulum has swung from a complete inattention to worship to a total immersion in a new industry.

But with all this fuss about worship, what has really changed? Well, we have numerous big churches. Services are much slicker than they used to be. Musicians, songwriters, and worship leaders are everywhere. Media and technology have become the servants of worship in many places.

But something seems to be wrong, out of kilter, maybe. People are fighting over worship, churches are breaking up, and some pastors and musicians can't wait to get out of this three-ring circus!

So why would anyone want to throw another book on this growing pile of "Here's how to grow a successful church through worship" craze?

Good question. I asked it too.

But wait. Don't throw Kevin Navarro's book on that pile. It is different.

He isn't saying, "Here's a new style, a new gimmick, a new hook, a new come-on."

No. His whole approach is to give your community a taste of the kingdom of God. The church doesn't deliver goods, products, or things. Instead, not just the songs we sing but also the hospitality, the atmosphere, the teaching, the Eucharist—all these and more constitute a taste of heaven.

This is a book for those who know that something is wrong about the way we are doing our worship. If you want to get off the consumer track and "do truth," then this book will help you reverse the trend and go in a direction that is more satisfying to the soul because it gets to the heart of what worship is all about.

Robert E. Webber
Myers Professor of Ministry
Director of M.A. in Worship and Spirituality
Northern Seminary
Lombard, Illinois

ACKNOWLEDGMENTS

I want to thank Robert N. Hosack and Baker Publishing Group for the opportunity to write this follow-up book to *The Complete Worship Leader*. I want to thank Dave Kurz for always talking about heaven. His influence permeates this work. Thanks to the Bethany Evangelical Free Church staff, elder council, and ministry team leaders for creating a place of truth, hope, and purpose for all people. I want to thank Jon Swanson and the creative arts team at Bethany: Jada Swanson, Stacey Kasper, Suzanne Gasaway, Warren Lotter, and Traci Lotter. It's an inspiration to create the complete worship service with you every week. Your creative spirit is a reverent eccentricity mixed with God-infused beauty. I want to thank everyone who read this manuscript to make it a better book: Susan Navarro, Nancy Johnson, Roy Sturgeon, Matthew Arnold, Mike Harrison, Cheryl Johnson, Reg Grant, and the creative arts team. I also want to thank my editor at Baker Books, Kelley Meyne. A special thanks to Bob Webber, Craig Blomberg, Leith Anderson, Nancy Beach, Robb Redmann, Michael Card, and Sally Morganthaler. I want to thank my beautiful wife, Susan, for her faithful love and encouragement. Thanks to my kids for all the fun and laughter. Thanks to my mom and dad for always encouraging me to dream and to do what I love. A special thanks to my heavenly Father for inviting me to be a part of his family. I never imagined how wonderful the body of Christ would be. I'm looking forward to the wedding banquet at the end of the age to discover who else is in this amazing family.

INTRODUCTION

The Complete Worship Service is a follow-up book to *The Complete Worship Leader* (Baker Books, 2001). Whereas *The Complete Worship Leader* focused on the development of the person leading worship, *The Complete Worship Service* discusses the elements of a dynamic worship service. I believe that every complete worship service is a dress rehearsal for the wedding banquet at the end of the age.

I have lightheartedly said on many occasions that churches grow like restaurants grow. Well, this statement is actually quite true. The essence of the complete worship service is hospitality. An invitation is given, an environment is experienced, a meal is tasted, and then people talk about the experience.

I believe that healthy churches are filled with people in the habit of inviting family, friends, and neighbors to church because they anticipate something exciting happening. Once these guests arrive, warm and hospitable people make them feel at home. Furthermore, the ambiance provokes a sense of wonder. Then a delicious meal is served through Christ-centered worship with the following ingredients: artistic expression (including music), the preaching of the Word, and the celebrating of the Eucharist. After people experience this taste of heaven, they leave and talk about the experience; talking about the experience consummates the joy.

The complete worship service is a contemporary version of the description of ancient worship: call to worship, Word, Eucharist, and mission. I describe a worship service as an act of hospitality, as a good restaurant, as having someone over to your home for dinner and all the preparation associated with it, to help the modern reader relate this culinary metaphor to the spiritual reality of the kingdom of God.

In this book I will share how we need to emphasize the Good News, not the "good advice" that is so prevalent in worship services today. People are longing for the gospel in our worship services.

I believe this book will change the future of worship around the world as we discover the power of hospitality through Christ-centered worship.

As we ponder practical ways to create the complete worship service, never forget the power of prayer and the preaching of Christ. Everything I am about to share must be immersed in intercessory prayer as we cry out to God to heal our communities. Every detail about how to invite a person to church must be prefaced by remembering that only the preaching of Jesus Christ and the power of the Holy Spirit will anchor anything I say in the following chapters in spiritual effectiveness. May God richly bless you as you give your community a foretaste of heaven this weekend.

PART ONE

LONGING FOR A
TASTE OF HEAVEN

one

LONGING FOR HEAVEN

THE PURSUIT OF HAPPINESS

The search for happiness is one of the chief sources of unhappiness.[1] As I write, millions of people are spending money trying to find happiness. Someone is buying a cup of coffee, purchasing a new pair of shoes, trying out a religion, or joining a health club because he or she thinks that this is the key to happiness. Someone is taking a cruise or going out to eat in order to taste happiness, even if it is for only a few moments.

People pursue unhealthy relationships because they think those relationships will bring them happiness. Who knows? This other person might bring happiness. There is a deep emptiness inside the soul, and maybe another person can fulfill this deep need. Sofia Coppola's movie *Lost in Translation* portrays two very lonely people looking for companionship. It doesn't quite matter what they do—karaoke, barhopping, video games—as long as they have companionship.[2] People are dying to find happiness. "'Meaningless! Meaningless!' says the Teacher. 'Utterly meaningless! Everything is meaningless'" (Eccles. 1:2).

Why is it that we feel so empty and unfulfilled? Why is it that after spending all that money, we feel cheated and ripped off? Why did that experience not bring happiness? Calvin Miller once said, "The world is poor because her fortune is buried in the sky and all her treasure maps are of the earth."[3] Herein lies the heart of the issue. The problem is not our pursuit of happiness but the pursuit of happiness in earthly treasures. Our energy is expended every day pursuing happiness from undependable sources. We are literally running the wrong marathon. No wonder we are so exhausted. Seven days a week, fifty-two weeks a year, year after year, we wholeheartedly pursue substitutes that never deliver. Maurice Sendak said, "There must be more to life than having everything."[4]

THE LURE OF ADVERTISING

Companies spend millions of dollars telling us how unhappy we are and that what we need is what they are selling. People have graduate degrees in how to manipulate our existential dilemma. The right phrase and the right look are all designed to fuel our unhappiness. This high-tech unhappiness mantra infuses the human soul. We believe the lie, and we embrace reckless idolatry. In *Dangers, Toils, and Snares*, John Ortberg writes:

> When we take our children to the shrine of the Golden Arches, they always lust for the meal that comes with a cheap little prize, a combination christened, in a moment of marketing genius, the Happy Meal. You're not just buying fries, McNuggets, and a dinosaur stamp; you're buying happiness. Their advertisements have convinced my children they have a little McDonald-shaped vacuum in their souls: "Our hearts are restless till they find their rest in a happy meal." . . .
>
> The problem with the Happy Meal is that the happy wears off, and they need a new fix. No child discovers lasting happiness in just one: "Remember that Happy Meal? What great joy I found there!" Happy Meals bring happiness only to Mc-

Donalds. You ever wonder why Ronald McDonald wears that grin? Twenty billion Happy Meals, that's why. When you get older, you don't get any smarter; your happy meals just get more expensive.[5]

Our adult happy meals can be so expensive that we end up in debt, paying outrageous percentages on credit cards. Then when we max out our credit cards, we begin the surfing game. We surf from one card to another as the new card gives us an introductory low percentage rate. Then when we get sick of that, we look into second mortgages so we can lump all our expensive happy meals into one payment. We waste ourselves on materialism and, like drug addicts, realize that we traded valuable resources for temporary pleasure. We bury ourselves one shovelful at a time.[6] That is how materialism works. It is addictive. The same is true for sex, work, and anything else we think will bring us life. "All who make idols are nothing, and the things they treasure are worthless" (Isa. 44:9).

The bottom line is that nothing in this world will offer lasting satisfaction. If you think this proposition is false, you have already embraced the essence of idolatry. We are told in Romans 1 that God's creative acts have produced naturalists and materialists, not theists and certainly not Christians. General revelation condemns us. Yes, God created the universe. Yes, the likely response should be worship. However, we have not worshiped the living God; we have worshiped the creation. Until we realize how strong this false worship is, we will never realize our purpose in this life. For, you see, we are all worshipers. The question is not *are* we worshiping but *what* are we worshiping? And when we worship anything other than God, our gratitude is misguided. Scott Hafemann states:

> The essence of sin is *misguided* gratitude, not ingratitude. As dependent creatures we all, by nature, thank somebody or something (usually ourselves!) for what we experience and

19

achieve. And the ultimate object of our gratitude becomes the object of our worship. In turn, the object of our gratitude becomes the object of our service, since we inevitably serve whatever or whomever we think will meet our needs (see Matthew 6:24). This is why, in Romans 1:25, worship and service are linked together: the object of our worship always becomes the master of our behavior. This is a law of human nature, inasmuch as God made us to worship and live for him. The sin of idolatry, whether in the age-old worship of nature or in the modern worship of ourselves, is consequently the same: worshiping and serving the creature rather than the Creator (see Romans 1:25).[7]

Those of us who are collectors know the pull of misguided gratitude. As long as I can remember, I have been collecting something. From the time I was a teenager on through my college years, I was a jazz record collector. I still have the vinyl today. Every time Miles Davis experimented with a new sound and produced a new album, I was the first to buy it. Then it was important to make sure I owned all of the Prestige recordings. Then the Columbia years . . . yes, I had to own the Columbia years as well! This process was duplicated with Louis Armstrong, Count Basie, Duke Ellington, Charlie Parker, Dizzy Gillespie, Clifford Brown, Dexter Gordon, John Coltrane, Thelonious Monk, Freddie Hubbard, and a score of others whose names could fill another book.

The same is true for you. Maybe you are a book collector and you cannot wait to add the latest edition of the Library of America to your collection. Or maybe you collect DVDs and you cannot wait for the next new release to add to your collection. What in the past was easily accessible at a rental store or even free at the local library is now consumed like vanilla lattes at Starbucks. DVDs are big business for the film industry. Why? It is because human beings are driven by emotional impulse to satisfy a deep longing in their souls for fulfillment.

I have a plaque on my wall that says, "The Best Things in Life Are Not Things." Although we as artists tend to lean toward Epicureanism (knowledge is derived from the physical senses), we need to remember what Saint Augustine said: "Our hearts are restless until they find their rest in Thee." We should enjoy what God has created, and, yes, we should give him thanks. But we need to be careful that we do not turn a vertical longing into a horizontal pursuit. We need to guard our worldview to ensure that it does not turn from theism to naturalism. The operative word is *worship*.

WHAT WE LONG FOR IS A TASTE OF HEAVEN

We behave like this because we are ultimately pursuing heaven. This is true for all human beings, whether they know it or not. And as believers, we are resident aliens who belong to another country: the kingdom of God. We are like amphibians caught between two worlds. And the world in which we will find the most satisfaction is the kingdom of God.

This, in fact, is *the issue* of the people coming into our churches week after week. Whether guests or returning members, people have been trying to get a fix like drug addicts all week long when what they are really searching for is a taste of heaven. This is true of believers and unbelievers.

God has put eternity in their hearts.

Now we know that if the earthly tent we live in is destroyed, we have a building from God, an eternal house in heaven, not built by human hands. Meanwhile we groan, longing to be clothed with our heavenly dwelling, because when we are clothed, we will not be found naked. For while we are in this tent, we groan and are burdened, because we do not wish to be unclothed but to be clothed with our heavenly dwelling, so that what is mortal may be swallowed up by life. Now it is God who has made us for this very purpose and has given us the Spirit as a deposit, guaranteeing what is to come.

2 Corinthians 5:1–5

So the questions are these: What will people get when they come to our churches this weekend? Will we satisfy their longing for heaven? Will we give them a taste of the wedding banquet at the end of the age? I believe that is exactly what the complete worship service is intended to do. Anything short of that would be like going to a fine steak restaurant only to be served Hamburger Helper for your main course. You did not get what you were longing for.

The complete worship service should be designed to remind us that there are reasons God said, "You shall have no other gods before me." The theological reason for this commandment is that God is jealous. The existential reason for this prohibition of idolatry is lack of fulfillment. Idolatry does not deliver the goods. Serving another does not bring happiness because "the greatest things in life are not things." And the best resolution to this slogan is to give your community a taste of the kingdom of God. Let them taste and see that the Lord is good. Give them a longing for the wedding banquet at the end of the age.

But our citizenship is in heaven. And we eagerly await a Savior from there, the Lord Jesus Christ, who, by the power that enables him to bring everything under his control, will transform our lowly bodies so that they will be like his glorious body.

Therefore, my brothers, you whom I love and long for, my joy and crown, that is how you should stand firm in the Lord, dear friends!

Philippians 3:20–4:1

22

NEVER FULFILLED UNTIL HEAVEN

We must remember that although we can have a taste of heaven in this world, we will never be satisfied until we enter the fullness of the kingdom. I realize that there are different theological positions on this issue. Indeed, some believe we can experience the fullness of the kingdom in this world. I think this interpretation is fallacious. I identify more with the apostle Paul when he said:

> We know that the whole creation has been groaning as in the pains of childbirth right up to the present time. Not only so, but we ourselves, who have the firstfruits of the Spirit, groan inwardly as we wait eagerly for our adoption as sons, the redemption of our bodies. For in this hope we were saved. But hope that is seen is no hope at all. Who hopes for what he already has? But if we hope for what we do not yet have, we wait for it patiently.
>
> Romans 8:22–25

This world is experiencing labor pains, and there is no anesthesiologist on duty. I am the father of four boys and one girl. My wife is the one who experienced the reality of Romans 8. I tried to play the good coach who pretended I knew what she was going through. We men do not have a clue. The closest experience to childbirth we might have is passing a kidney stone. My wife wanted to be Superwoman and go all natural with our firstborn. By the time she reached five centimeters, she was screaming for an epidural. Are you kidding? When I saw the final stages of Timothy's birth, I thought to myself, *I would not have asked for an epidural. I would have asked for someone to knock me out!* Labor is *painful.*

As glorious as our worship services can be, we need to remember that even in the most holy place on earth, creation is still in labor. We can taste of the kingdom, but the final consummation is yet to be experienced. The fullness of the kingdom of God is not yet here. We still await our glorious hope. The complete worship service is created to help us long each week for what is yet to come. That is what the rest of this book is all about. Press on!

HEAVEN

HEAVEN IS MY HOME

As an adult, I have positive childhood memories. I know some of you will gloss over what I am about to say because this was not your childhood experience. Bear with me. The first neighborhood I grew up in was the kind of neighborhood where you could roam the streets, in and out of other people's yards, in and out of your friends' homes, and this was normal. It was simply a part of the culture that adults expected there would be kids from the neighborhood in their houses.

I vividly remember playing with my friends and having the time of my life. There was no rush to grow up. Being a kid was fun, and it was as though we were suspended in time. In some ways, it seemed as though we could play for hours without a care in the world.

Yet, as much as I enjoyed playing in the neighborhood, there was nothing as sweet as coming home. My home was a very warm home, a place of rest. Sure, I had chores. Actually, as an only child, I had double duty: cleaning the inside and outside of the house. And my mom was the kind of mom who when she was teaching you how to make a bed, would tear it up a dozen times until you had your corners perfectly tucked in and the bedspread iron-tight perfect. Yet there was a lot of love in this house.

As a kid, I loved coming home and watching *Scooby-Doo*, *Gilligan's Island*, and *The Flintstones*. I loved smelling the homemade Mexican food my mom was cooking. Some days it was calabasitas and taquitos. Other days it was sour-cream enchiladas. And then there was my favorite: pork green chili with pinto beans. My dad used to say, "Chili kills the germs, and beans kick 'em out." Laughter was another important aspect of my childhood.

Furthermore, my mom and dad were very cool parents. They were in softball leagues and bowling leagues, loved to dance, and listened to Sam Cook, Fats Domino, and the Platters. In my home, it was the fun, the smell of home-cooked meals, the music, the art, the order, and most importantly, the love that I remember most.

I suspect that when we get to heaven, there will be music and a home-cooked meal like we have never tasted before. As much as I love my mom's Mexican cooking, I get the idea that the meal that is awaiting our arrival will be so delicious that we will realize then why God never allowed us complete satisfaction in this world.

The music will be so joyful and the hearts so grateful that this will be like no party we have ever experienced. Listening to Fats Domino and the Platters will have been but a minor prelude to the doo-wop we will experience in heaven. If the fruit of the Spirit is joy and in the presence of the Lord there is fullness of joy, count on it, friend: this will be a party with lots of joy and joyful songs.

> Shout for joy to the LORD, all the earth.
>   Worship the Lord with gladness;
>   come before him with joyful songs.
> Know that the LORD is God.
>   It is he who made us, and we are his;
>   we are his people, the sheep of his pasture.

Enter his gates with thanksgiving
  and his courts with praise;
  give thanks to him and praise his name.
For the LORD is good and his love endures forever;
  his faithfulness continues through all generations.

Psalm 100:1–5

Heaven is our home. And whether you had a good or bad childhood, you do not want to miss this home-cooked meal—the wedding banquet—prepared for all who have been called according to his purpose. Heaven will be a home where friendship and family are a perpetual holiday, a place with time to spend enjoying each other's company and maybe even enjoying a good cup of heavenly coffee. I also think there will be lots of laughter in that place.

> Author and professor Lewis Smedes used to ask his students if they wanted to go to heaven when they died. Everyone would raise a hand. Then he'd ask, "Be honest now—who would like to go *today*?" A few would raise their hands slowly, giving what they thought was the correct answer, looking around to see if they were the only ones. They were. Most people wanted a rain check. They were ready to die—just not today. Then Professor Smedes would ask who would like to see the world set straight once and for all tomorrow: "No more common colds, no more uncommon cancers. Hungry people would have plenty; no one would lift a finger to harm another; we would be at peace with everyone, even with ourselves. Anybody interested in that?" There would be a frenzy of hand-lifting. Then Smedes would point out that if that new world is what you really want, then heaven's where you'd like to be.[1]

I think that many of us are just like the students in Lewis Smedes's class. We are not quite sure about leaving earth today, but we long for a place where there will be no more pain, no more war, no more divorce. Friends, the name of that place is heaven. That is why we long for heaven. That is why we pursue even a taste of heaven on this earth. By the way, Dr. Smedes went home to be with the Lord a few years ago and is enjoying what he taught at Fuller Seminary. We will all soon catch up with him and will then wonder why we were not more excited about getting to that place sooner.

"I Can't Get No Satisfaction"

We must realize that we will never be satisfied with this world. I mean, how many rock-and-roll songs are there that try to say this very thing? Of course I'm thinking of the famous Rolling Stones song "I Can't Get No Satisfaction." U2 laments, "I still haven't found what I'm looking for." We must have a theology of contentment; we must remember that we will never find jam-packed satisfaction in this world. Undoubtedly, we can have a taste of heaven and enjoy God's creation, but we will never be completely satisfied until we experience the jubilation of the kingdom perfected. The preacher in Ecclesiastes put it this way:

> I thought in my heart, "Come now, I will test you with plea-sure to find out what is good." But that also proved to be meaningless. "Laughter," I said, "is foolish. And what does pleasure accomplish?" I tried cheering myself with wine, and embracing folly—my mind still guiding me with wisdom. I wanted to see what was worthwhile for men to do under heaven during the few days of their lives.
>
> I undertook great projects: I built houses for myself and planted vineyards. I made gardens and parks and planted all kinds of fruit trees in them. I made reservoirs to water groves of flourishing trees. I bought male and female slaves and had other slaves who were born in my house. I also owned more herds and flocks than anyone in Jerusalem before me. I amassed silver and gold for myself, and the treasure of kings and provinces. I acquired men and women singers, and a harem as well—the

delights of the heart of man. I became greater by far than anyone in Jerusalem before me. In all this my wisdom stayed with me.

I denied myself nothing my eyes desired;
   I refused my heart no pleasure.
My heart took delight in all my work,
   and this was the reward for all my labor.
Yet when I surveyed all that my hands had done
   and what I had toiled to achieve,
everything was meaningless, a chasing after the wind;
   nothing was gained under the sun.

Ecclesiastes 2:1–11

What I hear this preacher saying is that he went through life like a teenager goes through an all-you-can-eat buffet. There is so much to enjoy on this earth, but it will never bring satisfaction. We were made to dine in another world. And if we derive any pleasure in this world, it is but a foretaste of what is to come. It is merely to whet our appetites. Heaven will be more fulfilling than any earthly pleasure. This is why Jesus told us to "seek first his kingdom and his righteousness" (Matt. 6:33).

IN HIS PRESENCE IS FULLNESS OF JOY

Psalm 16:11 declares, "You have made known to me the path of life; you will fill me with joy in your presence, with eternal pleasures at your right hand." And Psalm 21:6 says, "Surely you have granted him eternal blessings and made him glad with the joy of your presence." We are told again and again that the presence of the Lord brings joy. In the New Testament we are told that the empirical evidence of the Holy Spirit invading a human heart is joy (Gal. 5:22–23).

In our pursuit of fulfillment, we need to go to the source: the Shekinah glory of God. People need to experience the power

29

of the Holy Spirit in our churches. We should be crying out to God through prayer every week that he will show up at our churches and manifest his presence in our midst. What we offer our communities is not only hope in Jesus but also the by-product of that hope: contentment. And since it is only in the presence of the Lord that there is fullness of joy, the key to jubilation is to be immersed in a relationship with the Father through Jesus Christ. This is one of the most significant by-products of the complete worship service.

The reality is that the local church has exactly what the seeker is looking for: joy. Remember, when two or three gather together in his name, he is there in their midst (Matt. 18:20). And if people with this existential longing come to church and encounter the living God, they will find the source of contentment. The frenzied pursuit they go through every day can find fulfillment in the Lord's presence.

So what we have to offer every weekend is a taste of heaven. If heaven is where the presence of the Lord will be experienced in its fullness, then the complete worship service should be the place where there is a foretaste of heaven.

THE HEAVENLY BANQUET

In heaven there will be a wedding banquet. It will be pure *kairos* (not chronological time, but experiential time), chockfull of joy, laughter, and celebration by the King's kids from every tribe, tongue, and nation. It will be a time of worshiping the King of Kings and the Lord of Lords. It will be the new and improved complete worship service. Therefore, every worship service until then must be a foreshadowing of this time that the Bible refers to as our glorious hope.

To remember that a wedding banquet has in fact been prepared, ponder this sobering passage of Scripture in Matthew 22:2–14:

The kingdom of heaven is like a king who prepared a wedding banquet for his son. He sent his servants to those who had been invited to the banquet to tell them to come, but they refused to come.

Then he sent some more servants and said, "Tell those who have been invited that I have prepared my dinner: My oxen and fattened cattle have been butchered, and everything is ready. Come to the wedding banquet."

But they paid no attention and went off—one to his field, another to his business. The rest seized his servants, mistreated them and killed them. The king was enraged. He sent his army and destroyed those murderers and burned their city.

Then he said to his servants, "The wedding banquet is ready, but those I invited did not deserve to come. Go to the street corners and invite to the banquet anyone you find." So the servants went out into the streets and gathered all the people they could find, both good and bad, and the wedding hall was filled with guests.

But when the king came in to see the guests, he noticed a man there who was not wearing wedding clothes. "Friend," he asked, "how did you get in here without wedding clothes?" The man was speechless.

Then the king told the attendants, "Tie him hand and foot, and throw him outside, into the darkness, where there will be weeping and gnashing of teeth."

For many are invited, but few are chosen.

Now, in this story there are some important details about the wedding banquet. First of all, the father prepared the banquet for the son. Secondly, we are told that the servants went out twice: prior to the day of the wedding banquet and on the wedding day. Next, we are told that the invitation was rejected by the recipients.

What we need to understand about this story is that refusal to come to the wedding banquet was a statement of disrespect toward the king and his son. This was a rejection of the appointed king. It was a statement of political uprising. This was not just "No, thanks. I'm busy this week" but "I refuse to subordinate myself to the rightful heir of the throne."

The invitation was so violently rejected that some of the king's servants were killed. The king was outraged. The king had these disrespectful people and their city destroyed. In response to this insubordination and disrespect from the somebodies, the king invited the nobodies to join him at this celebration. The text tells us that the wedding hall was filled. An invitation went out to many, but some rejected the invitation and others accepted. It is in this context that the passage announces, "Many are invited, but few are chosen."

The invitation to come to the wedding banquet is still going out today. All of us have been called to distribute this message. We have been chosen by God to go and communicate this glorious news. I personally believe that every weekend when we gather together, we are the servants inviting once again.

We put out the word when we preach the gospel. We announce the wedding banquet through the music and the arts. We announce the wedding banquet when we come around the Lord's Table. The complete worship service is a weekly platform to invite all to the wedding and to begin to taste and see that the Lord is good.

We want to give people a foretaste of this glorious wedding banquet. We want them to anticipate the day when we will be with every tribe and nation in the presence of the Lord forever. As we continue to process how this relates to the local church, we must remember that this is what our community is longing for: a taste of heaven. This taste of heaven, the essence of the complete worship service, is what our next chapter will address in detail.

three

A TASTE OF HEAVEN, THE WORSHIP SERVICE

God gives us a taste of heaven when we worship with the body of Christ. We celebrate with God's people what Christ has done for us. We momentarily transcend the ordinary and experience the extraordinary: the manifest presence of God. The complete worship service creates an anticipation of what eternity with Christ will be like. We are proclaiming that we have an inheritance that has not yet been fully revealed. We are reminded through the singing of our songs, the preaching of our sermons, and the celebrations around the table of the glorious future God has in store for us. Listen to the way Peter describes this truth:

> Praise be to the God and Father of our Lord Jesus Christ! In his great mercy he has given us new birth into a living hope through the resurrection of Jesus Christ from the dead, and into an inheritance that can never perish, spoil or fade—kept in heaven for you, who through faith are shielded by God's power until the coming of the salvation that is ready to be revealed in the last time. In this you greatly rejoice, though now for a little while you may have had to suffer grief in all kinds of trials. These have come so that your faith—of greater worth

than gold, which perishes even though refined by fire—may be proved genuine and may result in praise, glory and honor when Jesus Christ is revealed. Though you have not seen him, you love him; and even though you do not see him now, you believe in him and are filled with an inexpressible and glorious joy, for you are receiving the goal of your faith, the salvation of your souls.

1 Peter 1:3–9

Peter reminds his readers that we have a living hope through the resurrection of Jesus Christ. We have an inheritance that can never perish, spoil, or fade, and this inheritance is kept in heaven for us. Our inheritance is the fullness of God's presence as an experienced reality. This is what we need to be talking about when we come together in worship.

I am convinced that our Christianity has become so anchored in the temporal that we have forgotten that we are citizens of another world. We are heirs in the kingdom of God. We shall reign with Christ forever and ever. The more our worship services provide a taste of heaven, the more our worship services will be *complete*. The more our worship services give us a taste of this world, the more they will be *incomplete*.

Because God has created us in his image, we are forever longing for another world. We long for the world where God dwells. We long to know not only that God is omnipresent but also that we will experience his manifest presence as soon as possible. Our great joy in this world is that heaven and earth seem to collide occasionally. This, in fact, was the case on the day of Pentecost.

The more our worship services anticipate heaven, the more centered they will be. The more our worship services give us a taste of heaven and not merely a lecture on heaven, the more our worship services will be filled with hope. And the more our worship services collide with the place where God dwells, the more our churches will exemplify eternity.

CELEBRATING WHAT CHRIST HAS DONE

In a very riveting way, we not only anticipate heaven but also thrill in our citizenship in heaven. Christ has made this possible. You see, we not only have a song to sing, we have a reason to sing. Christ is our theme. Christ is the subject in our preaching. Christ is the order of service.

When we celebrate what Christ has done, we are doing what the residents of heaven do in the book of Revelation. One of the keys to interpreting Revelation is to look at the songs. Notice the lyrical content:

> In the center, around the throne, were four living creatures, and they were covered with eyes, in front and in back. The first living creature was like a lion, the second was like an ox, the third had a face like a man, the fourth was like a flying eagle. Each of the four living creatures had six wings and was covered with eyes all around, even under his wings. Day and night they never stop saying:
>
> *"Holy, holy, holy*
> *is the Lord God Almighty,*
> *who was, and is, and is to come."*

Whenever the living creatures give glory, honor and thanks to him who sits on the throne and who lives for ever and ever, the twenty-four elders fall down before him who sits on the throne, and worship him who lives for ever and ever. They lay their crowns before the throne and say:

> "You are worthy, our Lord and God,
>   to receive glory and honor and power,
> for you created all things,
>   and by your will they were created
>   and have their being."

Then I saw in the right hand of him who sat on the throne a scroll with writing on both sides and sealed with seven seals. And I saw a mighty angel proclaiming in a loud voice, "Who is worthy to break the seals and open the scroll?" But no one in heaven or on earth or under the earth could open the scroll or even look inside it. I wept and wept because no one was found who was worthy to open the scroll or look inside. Then one of the elders said to me, *"Do not weep! See, the Lion of the tribe of Judah, the Root of David, has triumphed. He is able to open the scroll and its seven seals."*

Then I saw a Lamb, looking as if it had been slain, standing in the center of the throne, encircled by the four living creatures and the elders. He had seven horns and seven eyes, which are the seven spirits of God sent out into all the earth. He came and took the scroll from the right hand of him who sat on the throne. And when he had taken it, the four living creatures and the twenty-four elders fell down before the Lamb. Each one had a harp and they were holding golden bowls full of incense, which are the prayers of the saints. And they sang a new song:

> "You are worthy to take the scroll
>   and to open its seals,
> because you were slain,
>   and with your blood you purchased men for God
>   from every tribe and language and people and nation.
> You have made them to be a kingdom and priests to serve
>   our God,
>   and they will reign on the earth."

Revelation 4:6–5:10, italics added

There is an all-out celebration in heaven, and the residents of heaven are celebrating what the Lamb of God has done. This is the key to the complete worship service—Christ-centered worship. Everything is drawn together around a celebration of what Christ has done for us. This indeed is a taste of heaven, for this is what we will be doing in heaven.

The quickest way for worship services to degenerate into humanism is to remove Christ from the chorus. Once we start singing about us, the focus is distorted. This might be prayer, but it is not praise. Now, we need prayer, lots of it, but we also need to live in the understanding of what Christ has already done for us. We must be more Christ-centered in our worship services.

When it comes to our songs, we must be concerned about the theology in the lyrics. We must choose and write songs with theologically anchored lyrical content. Our songs need to retell the Jesus story. If you want to see power reenter your worship services, just start singing about Jesus again.

Furthermore, our preaching needs to celebrate Christ. The more I think of my preaching as an act of worship and not merely as an act of exhortation, the more gospel I will have in my messages. Teach the Bible, but for heaven's sake, preach Christ. The pulpit is not the place to share ideologies and opinions but the place to gossip the gospel. Declare the mighty acts of God.[1]

Also, we need to reintroduce consistent celebration of the Lord's Table in our worship services so that we can celebrate Christ more. When we make the decision to celebrate communion on a consistent basis, we will discover that our worship services end up being Christ-centered. This is why Eucharist has been the climax in the Catholic mass over the centuries.

CELEBRATING WITH HIS PEOPLE

Another element that will make our worship services a foretaste of heaven is the experience of celebrating with the people of God. The complete worship service is not just an individual experience. It is not just about our personal relationship with Jesus Christ. It is about a celebration that happens with the redeemed of the Lord. In their book *Resident Aliens*, Hauerwas and Willimon state:

> When we are baptized, we (like the first disciples) jump on a moving train. As disciples, we do not so much accept a creed, or come to a clear sense of self-understanding by which we know this or that with utter certitude. We become part of a journey that began long before we got here and shall continue long after we are gone. Too often, we have conceived of salvation—what God does to us in Jesus—as a purely personal decision, or a matter of finally getting our heads straight on basic beliefs, or of having some inner feelings of righteousness about ourselves and God, or of having our social attitudes readjusted. . . . We [Hauerwas and Willimon] argue that salvation is not so much a new beginning but rather a beginning in the middle, so to speak. Faith begins, not in discovery, but in remembrance. The story began without us, as a story of the peculiar way God is redeeming the world, a story that invites us to come forth and be saved by sharing in the work of a new people whom God has created in Israel and Jesus.[2]

One day we will experience a worship service with people from every ethnic background, for God has been redeeming people from every nation. One day we will experience a worship service with people from every generation, for God has been redeeming people from every generation. One day we will experience a worship service with people from every social class, for God has been redeeming people from every social class.

When we get to heaven, we will be surprised at the lack of homogeneity. I believe we will be surprised at the mix of people and the mix of worship styles represented. I think we will hear musical instruments we have never heard before and ask, "Where is that wonderful sound coming from?" And we will probably discover worship with pentatonic, harmonic minor, or diminished scales and chords. Personally, I hope some of it sounds like Louis Armstrong, Miles Davis, or John Coltrane.

There will not be separate worship services for builders, boomers, busters, and the emerging generations. Our people-blindness will be lifted, and we will see a child, worshiping with us for the very first time. We will see a senior citizen with a new appreciation. Our ears will echo with the words of a lady from Bangladesh shouting at the top of her lungs, "He is worthy! He is worthy!"

What we are certain of is that we will be worshiping with the body of Christ. It will be a celebration. Note that last sentence. I'll say it again. It *will be* a celebration. So put on your party shoes and pull out the tambourine. Get ready for some feasting. Get ready for some laughter. Get ready for heaven.

The best way I know to get ready for heaven is to engage in the discipline of celebration. And the best way to engage in the discipline of celebration is the complete worship service. Do not squander your next weekend service giving people good advice. Give them the Good News. Celebrate with the people of God what Christ has done. And foreshadow for your community the experience of heaven.

EXPERIENCING THE MANIFEST PRESENCE OF GOD

Then I saw a new heaven and a new earth, for the first heaven and the first earth had passed away, and there was no longer any sea. I saw the Holy City, the New Jerusalem, coming down out of heaven from God, prepared as a bride beautifully dressed for her husband. And I heard a loud voice from the throne saying, "Now the dwelling of God is with men, and he will live with them. They will be his people, and God himself will be with them and be their God. He will wipe every tear from their eyes. There will be no more death or mourning or crying or pain, for the old order of things has passed away."

Revelation 21:1–4

We are told in this wonderful passage that heaven is a place where the dwelling of God is with men and women. Heaven is described as the ultimate homecoming. It is where God's presence will be manifested and experienced in ways we have never known before. God is going to wipe every tear from our eyes. There will be no more death or mourning or crying or pain. Why? Because the way it used to be is no more. Heaven is an eradication of the old order. Heaven will be a place where nothing will interrupt our relationship with God. It will be like the original creation, before the fall, when humans experienced perfect fellowship with God.

The complete worship service is an experience of this atmosphere. It is a worship service where the presence of God is manifested in a special way. It is a worship service where there seems to be no interruption to our relationship with God. It is a time when we leave the cares of the world behind because we are getting a foretaste of the new order.

Now, hopefully, you understand that I am not minimizing the reality of our hardships in this world. I am simply saying that the complete worship service anticipates heaven, where there will be no more trials or hardships. It is so God-centered and Spirit-charged that it is as though we have entered another dimension. I believe this is how we should pray for our worship services. This is how we should program for our worship services. This is how we should preach in our worship services. This is how we should lead congregational singing, and this is how we should celebrate Eucharist.

ANTICIPATING BEING WITH CHRIST FOREVER AND EVER

When we pack for a trip, say a vacation, we pack only for the time frame in which we will be gone. We will pack some Woolite in anticipation that we will not have a washing machine. We will pack clothes we can mix and match. We will take the necessary amenities. But we are certain of one thing: we must not *overpack* or we will have to carry all of that stuff with us. And if we are going to an airport, we will not even make it on the airplane if we ignore the regulations for how much we are allowed to take.

Therefore, it is difficult for us to think of "packing" to go to a place from which we will never return to life as we now know it. We are not going there for just a couple of weeks. We are going to change our residency permanently. When we die or when the Lord returns, we will be with Christ forever and ever. This is our glorious hope.

Jesus told us that every time we celebrate the Lord's Table, we are not only remembering his blood shed for us but also proclaiming this truth until he comes. *Until he comes* is an important phrase. It says that every worship service has an end-of-the-age (eschatological) dimension to it. People should always leave our services remembering that the Lord will return and that his return has implications for how we should live. We need to convince the people of God that they are an eschatological community. Yes and amen! We are strangers in this world. Like the recipients of 1 Peter, we are resident aliens. Our home is not this earth.

When we gather together, may there always be anticipation that heaven is our home. May we long for this trip as much as we would long for a trip to Hawaii or Disneyland. AAA will not be able to help us out. The complete worship service gives us our road map for the journey ahead. We should anticipate this trip with great excitement. The purpose of the complete worship service is to spell out in detail for the body of Christ a chronicle of eternity. Through our sermons, music, and artistic expression, we must create hope that is rooted in a "the kingdom is here, but not yet" reality.

41

DRESS REHEARSAL FOR THE WEDDING BANQUET

In the performing arts, artists are familiar with dress rehearsals. After all the music has been rehearsed, after the blocking on the stage has been mapped out, after the lines to be spoken have been memorized, they run the whole production from start to finish as if it were the real deal. This is called a dress rehearsal.

The complete worship service is a dress rehearsal for the wedding banquet at the end of the age. After we run our rehearsals, after we learn our parts, after we memorize the music, after we practice our sermons, we must remember that the real deal is not Sunday. This next Sunday is but a dress rehearsal. Heaven is yet to come. But never forget, dress rehearsals run as though they were the actual performance.

Therefore, we must reflect on what the wedding banquet will be like. First of all, we are celebrating a marriage. Our celebration focuses on the Groom, Jesus Christ, and the bride, the body of Christ. We are celebrating our marriage vows. We are celebrating the covenant between Christ and his bride.

In the wedding banquet, we celebrate Christ's dedication to us. When Jesus said, "This is my body," he was saying, "My dedication to you is like the covenant established in the old days." In the ancient world, an animal was split for covenant parties to walk through, stating, "If I violate this covenant, may I be like this dead animal." Correlated with this, Jesus said, "This is my blood shed for sins." Again, this is a sign of the covenant he has made to us. These are the vows Jesus has made. This is what is celebrated at the wedding banquet.

The wedding celebration is the remembrance of what Christ committed to us. Furthermore, it is a celebration of the fact that Jesus kept his word. Divorce is so prevalent in our culture. But Jesus will never divorce us. He will never leave us. He will never forsake us. He will be with us till the end of the age.

This is his constant love for us. And the complete worship service is a celebration of this truth.

We will be celebrating with family and friends who have been invited to the wedding banquet. Typically, weddings include people other than the wedding party. The purpose of a wedding is to make a public declaration of the marriage. Well, the wedding banquet at the end of the age will be a public event. We will then worship with family and friends who have accepted Jesus Christ as Lord and Savior.

Our worship is not just individual expressions of gratitude. It is corporate worship. It is a community event. Our connection with our family and friends at our churches should be like a healthy family get-together. May we come to appreciate the body of Christ when we worship.

The next element of this wedding banquet is that there will be some people there you did not expect. When Susan and I got married, I had people I did not even know coming up to me and telling me that they were this cousin or that uncle of mine. I had no idea I had such a big family. Of course, any time you have a Hispanic wedding, *la familia* is a big deal. So it is in the body of Christ.

When we get to heaven, we will discover family members we never knew existed. We will meet brothers and sisters in Christ to whom we simply had no idea we were related. In the complete worship service, we should have a hospitable spirit toward every guest, for we do not know whom the Father is drawing.

The bottom line is that there will always be unbelievers in our midst who are about to become believers. The reason they are about to become believers is because the Father is drawing them. They are going to become believers through the work of the Spirit as they hear the preaching of the gospel. When all is said and done, all this is happening because God wants them to be among the attendees at the feast of his Son.

43

Finally, at the wedding banquet at the end of the age, we will celebrate. Yes, implied in the word *banquet* are food and drink. Implied in the phrase *wedding banquet* are music, dancing, and cheer. If the complete worship service is a dress rehearsal for the wedding banquet at the end of the age, I believe we have some major catching up to do in the area of celebration. Quite frankly, I am a bit confused that the very people who have come out of darkness into his wonderful light are the ones who are so conservative when it comes to declaring the praises of God. We have clear imperatives in the Word to praise the Lord with everything that is within us and with everything that God has created: musical instruments, singing, dance, feasting, and celebration.

We need to worship expressively without the concern of what others will think of us. We need to take off the girdle and live in the freedom that Christ died to give us. This is not just for charismatics or NFL fanatics. Our goal in worship should be to radically, passionately, wholeheartedly, and with great expression tell Jesus how much we love him and appreciate what he has done for us. I believe that this is what will be taking place in heaven.

The complete worship service is a foretaste of heaven. Every weekend we should anticipate the coming of Christ. After every worship service, we should celebrate the fact that he is alive forevermore, and consequently, so are we! After every worship service, people should leave our services with an anticipation of heaven. And in heaven there will be a wedding banquet. Notice how the arrival of the wedding banquet of the Lamb is described in Revelation:

> Then I heard what sounded like a great multitude, like the roar of rushing waters and like loud peals of thunder, shouting:
>
> "Hallelujah!
> For our Lord God Almighty reigns.

44

> Let us rejoice and be glad
>   and give him glory!
> For the wedding of the Lamb has come,
>   and his bride has made herself ready.
> Fine linen, bright and clean,
>   was given her to wear."
>
> (Fine linen stands for the righteous acts of the saints.)
>
> Then the angel said to me, "Write: 'Blessed are those who
> are invited to the wedding supper of the Lamb!'" And he
> added, "These are the true words of God."
>
> Revelation 19:6–9

The complete worship service is a pre-heaven celebration. The complete worship service is a dress rehearsal for that wedding banquet at the end of the age. The complete worship service is exactly what God's people need. Let us dig deeper into how to invite people to this experience.

45

PART TWO

PREPARING FOR A TASTE OF HEAVEN

four

QUALITY MATTERS

Creating a culture where people invite others to come to church starts with quality. In the same way that a good restaurant does business, the *quality* is the nonnegotiable. If you have a lovely atmosphere and the food is terrible, you have eliminated the possibility of customers ever returning. There is a French proverb that says, "There is no such thing as a pretty good omelet."

It has been said that for every positive experience, people tell one other person, and for every negative experience, they tell eleven. Now, if this is going on in your church, you have got to begin to improve the quality of your worship services. Stan Toler and Alan Nelson put it this way:

> We need to strive for excellence and care about our church property, programming and publicity because God deserves our best. We, as the local church, are His local franchise within a community. We represent Him. The Bible says that all Christians are to act as ambassadors, as liaisons between God and others. When we do things that reflect a shabby mind-set, we are certainly not representing Him well, because God does things with excellence. Look at creation. After everything was created, He looked at it and said, "It is good." When we offer mediocre music, have unfriendly ushers and ho-hum services,

and then present ourselves as a reflection of God's love and character, we insult Him.[1]

A Culture of Invitation

When you think of the quality of your worship experience, what impression comes to mind? Is it a positive or painful experience? If it is more painful, change must begin without delay. Make it your ambition to straighten out the quality of your worship services. "One thing about excellence, it's an exclusive club. And it's only for those who really want to pay dues."[2] Developing a culture of invitation begins with quality.

If people are going to invite others, they need to be confident that there is a low risk factor in your worship services. If there is instability in the quality of your worship service, people will not invite others; they are too embarrassed. They need to be unflinching in their confidence of what will take place next weekend.

Excellence Is Part of Western Culture

Why is quality control such an issue for Westerners? It is my own conviction that this is primarily a cultural phenomenon. Westerners demand quality. Whether they are purchasing a product or going to church, they expect quality and will not settle for second-rate experiences.

Every time our missionaries return from the field, I always ask them to identify what they notice about the church since they have left. The list is not that long, but it is significant. They always mention the friendliness of the people. Praise the Lord for that impression. Along with that, they say something to this effect: "I'm always reminded of how nice everything looks," or "The worship service is so professional yet worshipful." They tend to elaborate at this point on the resource challenges they face on the field when looking for musicians or equipment.

As I press them with this questioning, I discover that they notice not just the church but the entire geographical community. They mention the cleanliness of the neighborhood. They mention the quality of the restaurants. They mention the customer service in the local malls. Quality is expected in the American culture.

I have had my share of travel experience. I have been fortunate to travel to over forty countries. Although there are exceptions, there is generally not the cultural obsession for perfection in other countries like there is in America. In the United States, when you walk into a Starbucks, you would not think of waiting more than five minutes, on a busy day, to get a specialty cup of coffee. This is but one of many examples. Americans demand quality.

LEITH ANDERSON ON EVIDENCE OF EXCELLENCE

Leith Anderson, in his book *Leadership That Works: Hope and Direction for Church and Parachurch Leaders in Today's Complex World*, provides several bulleted items that show the epidemic of excellence in our culture:

- Black and white television . . . color television . . . high definition television
- Record albums . . . cassette tapes . . . compact discs
- Radios . . . portable radios . . . boom boxes . . . Sony Walkmans
- Telephones . . . long distance with operators . . . direct dial . . . touch-tone

51

- Expensive long distance ... cheap long distance ... Internet
- Slide rulers ... calculators ... computers ... personal computers ... laptops
- X-rays ... CT scans ... MRIs ... open MRIs
- 16mm movies ... color movies ... sound movies ... VCRs ... camcorders ... DVDs
- Carbon copies ... mimeograph ... photocopies
- Eyeglasses ... contact lenses ... vision correcting surgery
- Trains ... propeller planes ... jet planes ... jumbo jets ... supersonic jets
- U.S. mail ... special delivery ... FedEx (next day) ... fax (next minute)
- Cash ... checks ... credit cards ... ATMs and electronic banking
- Fountain pens ... ballpoint pens ... felt-tip pens ... palmtops

Anderson goes on to state:

The epidemic of excellence has not skipped the church or religious organizations. People expect church music to sound as good as the latest CD they bought, the local preacher to be as interesting as the radio preacher, the church newsletter to look as good as the company newsletter, the church building to be as well kept as the school building, church finances to be as carefully handled and reported as the bank's finances, the church secretary to answer the phone as courteously as the customer service representative at the mutual fund company, the climate in the sanctuary to be as comfortable as in the Wal-Mart store, the church sound system to be as clear as in the concert hall, and the Sunday School to be as much fun for children as Sesame Street.[3]

Anderson shares these observations from the angle of understanding the burden of pastoring a large church in our culture. Americans expect excellence. They expect quality. And when they come to church, they simply expect that the church will make the cultural adaptation and provide quality as well. While there is always the danger of becoming overly obsessed with this issue, I think that the church, regardless of the cultural expectation, should always put its best foot forward. I believe that it is honoring to God. "Do you see a man skilled in his work? He will serve before kings; he will not serve before obscure men" (Prov. 22:29).

Furthermore, we want to pray and plan for people to experience the taste of heaven we talked about earlier. We want the Holy Spirit to move in power this weekend. There is nothing as satisfying as meeting with God. That is the ultimate experience of quality. "Better is one day in your courts than a thousand elsewhere; I would rather be a doorkeeper in the house of my God than dwell in the tents of the wicked" (Ps. 84:10). Here are a few ways that we can improve the quality of our worship services.

IMPROVE THE QUALITY OF NURSERY FACILITIES

Every time my wife and I go on vacation, we visit other churches that are further along than our church is, simply for the purpose of collecting new ideas. I find it interesting that before I can even think about the worship service, I am thinking about one thing: getting my kids settled. Now that the kids are little older, they might just come with us to worship if we are running late. But when they were infants and toddlers, it was critical for us to make sure our little ones were going to be well cared for. We could not think of anything else until that issue was settled. Make sure the quality of your nursery facilities is top-notch if you want to attract guests with small children.

The first priority here is having an effective and efficient check-in system. It needs to be thorough but quick. There is nothing more frustrating than either the neglect of exchanging important information or the process taking too long. Remember, parents want to make it to the worship service. They have not come to your church primarily to experience the nursery; they have come to worship. The nursery needs to be thought of as a maidservant for the worship service.

Make sure allergy awareness and other medical concerns are dealt with in a professional manner. My son Aaron was born with all kinds of food allergies. His allergy to peanuts is a big concern. Every time we visit a church, I am still amazed that nurseries are stocked with peanut butter crackers of some sort. There are so many alternatives. One mistake and you could have a very sick kid on your hands—and, in some cases, a fatality. Make sure that parents like the Navarros are put at ease when they drop off their son with peanut allergies. This is all quality control.

Also, provide baby-changing stations in both the men's and women's restrooms. This is a move that says you love families with small children. By having baby changing stations in the restrooms, you also communicate excellence in your overall setting. This move is very impressive to young families.

Lastly, acquire a security pager system. This is a tremendous relief for parents. If there are problems, they can be contacted. By the way, if you have a nonvibrating pager system, you need to evaluate if projecting a number in the worship service to contact a parent is a distraction.

A quality nursery is important for the complete worship service. If you need to hire out, here is the place to do that. Spend your money on quality cribs, play equipment, monitor systems, and staffing for a five-star nursery. A quality nursery is critical for drawing worshipers.

Improve the Quality of the Music

Churches must also address the quality of the music they provide. Do you care about excellence? Do you care about getting it right? Do you care if your drummer cannot hold a groove? Do you care if the vocalist is singing out of tune? Or have you established a culture of mediocrity under the impression of being a caring and compassionate church? We need a culture of grace, but I do not see this as synonymous with mediocrity.

Some people will say, "But I am serving in a start-up church. I do not have a praise band. I have an organist and a trombone player." Or "We are not a large church. Therefore, we do not have a choir with really good vocalists. We are desperate; we will take anyone we can get."

If all you have is a guitar player and a vocalist, worship the Lord with everything that is within you. But as with preaching, I believe that improvement can be made not just with more inspiration but with more perspiration. Have that vocalist sing through every interval. Have him or her memorize the music. Have him or her rehearse one more time. Help him or her out by listening to recordings of the song. Put the extra effort in. In time, this will start to impact your musical culture. Never forget, musicians attract musicians, and good musicians attract good musicians. For more practical suggestions on musical tips, you might want to consult my first book, *The Complete Worship Leader*.

If you do not have anyone in your church with musical abilities, go to your knees and cry out to God to raise musicians in order to lead the body of Christ in worship. Ask the Lord to flood your church with artists. F. B. Meyer said, "The greatest tragedy in life is not un-answered prayer but un-offered prayer."[4] Never underestimate the role of petition and intercession as it pertains to building a worshiping community. God will do amazing things in response to your desperate cry for skilled musicians to lead your church in worship.

After you pray with fire about this issue, go into your community. Establish relationships with the best musicians. Give them the opportunity to play in your church, and if they are unchurched, lead them to Christ in the process. As I am writing this, I know a worship pastor who has established a relationship with an amazing professional drummer. This drummer comes in twice a month to play with their artists. In the meantime, the worship pastor is hanging out with him in coffee shops, telling him about Jesus Christ. This is in addition to him hearing the gospel every time he plays in a worship service. He is very open and will soon respond to the love of Christ.

At Bethany Evangelical Free Church, we build *on* commitment, not *toward* it. In other words, we try to deploy the gifts of those who are followers of Christ first and foremost. The exception is when an individual's destiny is on the line. We will do whatever we can to bring that individual into relationship with Christ. Now, you will obviously have to wrestle with this issue for your church. I must state that we would not invite musicians who are hostile to Christ to be on the team. But if they are teachable and they have the musical skills, we will definitely consider placing them in the rotation.

Challenge your musicians to keep on the edge. Have them study privately. Establish a culture of high expectations. Your culture will be established by what you permit. This is true in every other aspect of the local church as well. Make sure that your musicians are performing at their best. Make sure the arrangements work. Make sure the set is well thought through and there is a good flow. Work on the introductions and endings. Work on the transitions. Work on the modulations. Work on the tempos or the groove (not too fast, not too slow). Challenge your musicians to know when not to play. Music is comprised not only of sound but also of the absence of sound in time.

Like a good sports coach, keep them on the edge, playing their best game every week. Do not let them leverage the *V* word (*volunteer*). Remind them that there are excellent volunteer organizations in every community, and besides that, God has gifted and called them to serve *him* with excellence. George Bernard Shaw said, "Hell is full of musical amateurs."[5]

Any creative element you insert in your worship service requires a rehearsal and a run-through. We tend to think that only the music needs to be rehearsed. No! Rehearse the Scripture readings. Rehearse the testimonies. Rehearse the drama. Rehearse every element of your worship services. Then you need to have a run-through where transitions are executed and where the elements of the service are timed and edited appropriately for flow. Then by the time you get to the service, you will not have to use your first service as your run-through. You will have already had your run-through and will have made the adjustments prior to the service.

IMPROVE THE QUALITY OF THE TECHNOLOGY

Take the time to improve the quality of your technology and your technicians. Upgrade your sound, lighting, and computer systems just like you would your PC. Technology becomes dated very quickly. In every budget cycle, negotiate technological improvements. Acquire better cables, microphones, monitors, sound boards, speakers, amps, and system-enhancement equipment.

Upgrade your VCR to a DVD if you use film clips in your worship service. The picture quality is much better, not to mention the sound quality. Remember, God is in the details. All of these improvements will create an overall quality improvement people will appreciate.

Make sure you have the right people on your technical team. Go after a sound technician who has a musical ear, not just someone who loves to tweak knobs. The sound tech has to know what he or she is listening for. Find someone to run PowerPoint who can anticipate what needs to be up on the screen next. There is nothing more irritating than to be in a worship service and the PowerPoint slide is either one slide ahead or one slide behind. There needs to be some adrenaline at the back with the technicians; they need to be on the edge, anticipating what is happening on the platform.

Most importantly, provide the necessary training for your technicians. Bring in people from the outside to run seminars and perform on-the-job training. Require your technicians to attend these seminars. When there is local training for sound, lighting, or computer technology, have them attend. Put the expense in your budget. This has to be important to you. It is heartbreaking to spend all that time rehearsing music or preparing for a sermon only to show up on Sunday and discover the microphones not working, popping, distorted . . . you fill in the blank. Strive for the best quality you can afford in your equipment.

I want to say a word to small churches that can barely afford to pay a solo pastor. When it comes to technology, simply buy the best equipment you can afford. Again, using the restaurant metaphor, a restaurant does not have to be big to have good quality. The owners of the restaurant simply need to care about these issues and do what they can with the budget they have. I believe that quality has less to do with budgets and more to do with caring and conviction. Therefore, spend what you can to buy the best you can afford.

IMPROVE THE QUALITY OF PRAYER

One area that suffers neglect is the soaking of our worship services in prayer. Pray about every aspect of what is going to happen this weekend. Pray throughout the week that God will show up at your worship services. Pray that the Holy

Spirit will draw the body of Christ, as well as seekers from your community, to your church. Pray that he will speak to them in power and might.

We need to pray for God's leading in what to preach on and which songs to sing. We must pray about every detail of the worship services, including who should be on the platform. We must pray for the flow of the music portion of the worship service and that there will not be technical difficulties.

Pray prior to the worship services. At my church, our men's ministry has a rotation. These men pray before each of the worship services every week. I am convinced that the reason anything happens in our services is that God answers the prayers of these men and others who pray for God to do something supernatural. Another person who always prays through the worship service is my wife. I know that when I am preaching, Susan is sitting in the front row praying for God to move through me. Jim Cymbala said:

> If our churches don't pray, and if people don't have an appetite for God, what does it matter how many are attending the services? How would that impress God? Can you imagine the angels saying, "Oh, your pews! We can't believe how beautiful they are! Up here in heaven, we've been talking about them for years. Your sanctuary lighting—it's so clever. The way you have the steps coming up to the pulpit—it's wonderful. . . ." I don't think so.
>
> If we don't want to experience God's closeness here on earth, why would we want to go to heaven anyway? He is the center of everything there. If we don't enjoy being in his presence here and now, then heaven would not be heaven for us. Why would he send anyone there who doesn't long for him passionately here on earth?[6]

Finally, we need prayer teams after the services. We need people available to minister to others who need a word of encouragement or a healing touch. If you expect the Holy Spirit to move at your church, have people available to minister in response to the Word of God. Never underestimate the power of improving the quality of prayer as it pertains to dynamic worship services. Remember, if we want people to experience a taste of heaven, then God needs to be present. If God does not manifest his presence in the service, it will not be a taste of heaven but just another taste of earth.

Does quality matter? You better believe it. And never forget that you owe your best to Jesus Christ, who gave his best for you. "So whether you eat or drink or whatever you do, do it all for the glory of God" (1 Cor. 10:31). We strive for excellence first and foremost to please God, but we also strive for excellence because it matters to us. If getting better does not matter to you, put this book down and pray for God to inspire you to make a difference in your generation. Martin Luther King Jr. said, "If a man is called to be a street sweeper, he should sweep streets even as Michelangelo painted, or Beethoven composed music, or Shakespeare wrote poetry. He should sweep streets so well that all the hosts of heaven and earth will pause to say, here lived a great street sweeper who did his job well."[7]

And when we strive to please God and satisfy our own desire for excellence, the people we minister to will be the beneficiaries of really great worship experiences. The moment you give your very best week after week will be the moment you start an epidemic. People will begin to talk, and the buzz about your church will become contagious in the community. Whatever you do, never confuse quantity with quality. Whether you have a lot or a little, invest your best. The payoff will be big!

five

YOU'VE GOTTA BE THERE

After you have addressed the issue of your people not being embarrassed to invite guests to your church, create additional incentives for them to invite others. Of course, the greatest incentive is that you are giving guests an opportunity to experience life. Yet guests need to connect this real spiritual need with a felt need. The best way to address this is through special events, concerts, and message series. Your church needs a reason to say to its community, "You've gotta be at church this week."

One of the best compliments I received recently was when a member of our church said, "My wife and I were thinking of just skipping church last week, but the more we thought about it, the more we realized we didn't want to miss a worship service." He went on to say, "We love this church, we love our worship services, we love the music, we love the preaching, and we love what the Spirit of God is doing here."

Many of you have received similar encouragement. The key is that this enthusiasm needs to be epidemic. We need to turn attendees into advocates.[1] We need to create a culture in our churches where the best marketing will be word of mouth. The question we must ask is, what motivates anyone to tell someone else that they have got to be there?

Well, the answer to that question was partly addressed in the previous chapter. People are attracted to quality. They like excellence when they come to church. But in addition to quality, what else would motivate someone to say to a friend, "You've gotta be there"? Here are some suggestions.

FAITH STORIES

One way of motivating your people to invite others is to have them share their *faith stories*. I am indebted to Leith Anderson for this alternative term for the traditional word *testimonies*. The way the people at Wooddale Church define this term is this: "Faith Story is the spiritual autobiography of a Wooddaler who tells their personal story of coming to believe in Jesus Christ and choosing to follow him. Wooddale Church members and attendees are invited to tell their story. Faith Stories are given weekly at each of the weekend worship services with the exception of the weekend we celebrate Christian Communion."[2] To get an idea of what this could look like, visit www.wooddale.org, where samples of faith stories are posted under the heading "Wooddalers."

The key is to have people write out their faith stories. They will tell their stories with clarity if they are encouraged to write them out. Last week I was teaching on 1 Peter 3:1–7. This is the section about wives winning their unbelieving husbands over to the gospel by having a gentle and quiet spirit. This is also the section about husbands needing to honor their wives. Although I spent the sermon time talking about how this passage applies to us today, the moment of connection took place when I called a couple up to the platform.

Brian had become a follower of Jesus Christ the previous Easter. He shared about how he came to Christ following a car accident. During rehabilitation, his wife, Paula, was out of town over Good Friday and Easter weekend taking care of her mother, who had cancer. Paula asked him over the phone if he would read the Easter story to the kids in her absence. Afterward, he thumbed around in the children's Bible, looking for the Easter story, and finally found it. As the result of his reading the story, the Spirit of God convicted him and led him into a relationship with Jesus Christ.

He then went on to share how his wife influenced him not by pressuring him constantly to come to church but by being a loving example and honoring and respecting him. Their faith story was the ultimate illustration of the passage I was preaching on. I remember hearing Rick Warren say, "If I share, I'm the paid professional, but if a person in the congregation shares, they're the satisfied customer."

The faith story was also motivation for Brian and Paula to invite friends and family to church to hear their story. This is what happens when you schedule a faith story. The person giving the faith story will end up inviting others to worship. He or she will shift from being an attendee to being an advocate. This is exactly what happened in John 4:

> Many of the Samaritans from that town believed in him be-cause of the woman's testimony, "He told me everything I ever did." So when the Samaritans came to him, they urged him to stay with them, and he stayed two days. And because of his words many more became believers.
>
> They said to the woman, "We no longer believe just because of what you said; now we have heard for ourselves, and we know that this man really is the Savior of the world."
>
> John 4:39–42

If you begin to schedule faith stories on a regular basis, the enthusiasm and the sense that God is moving in your church will increase. This is important for morale. We tend to forget that God is moving in our local churches. Make opportunities to celebrate what he is doing.

Baptisms

Correlated with faith stories is baptism. When we experience a baptism, we experience the testimony of a new life. Along with experiencing new life, we experience the sense that God is moving in the church—tremendous motivation for worship.

People are looking for a church where God shows up. They long for the presence of the Lord. They are hungry for a taste of heaven. Remember, we are trying to offer a taste of heaven every weekend. When a church consistently experiences people coming to Christ, there is energy in the atmosphere. There is the sense that vibrant faith, not dead orthodoxy, is present "in the house."

At Bethany, our baptism services have resulted in some of the most memorable worship services we have ever had. When we expanded our church facility a few years ago, we had a mass baptism in our worship service. I had the privilege of baptizing my father and a dear friend who had come to Christ that year. The fun part was that we had pastors, moms, dads, and mentors all baptizing.

Occasionally, people will ask me why others, in addition to the pastoral staff, baptize. My reply is simply, "The Great Commission is for all believers of Jesus Christ, not just pastors, and part of the Great Commission is baptizing in the name of the Father, the Son, and the Holy Spirit." There is also a value statement made when others baptize. That statement is that everyone is on board with the Great Commission, and baptisms are the empirical evidence.

Every time a person is baptized, he or she invites family and friends to the service. We see our attendance go up when we have a baptism service. Depending on what you are trying to accomplish in your weekend services, baptisms might happen at another time. Maybe you have special baptism events. That is great. Keep it up! On the other hand, if you go through a year and no one has been baptized, go back to the drawing board and ask, "Is the Great Commission happening in this church?" If not, pray and plan for something to happen in the upcoming year. Start praying for a 10 percent conversion growth rate. This means if your weekend services average four hundred people, pray for forty people to make first-time decisions at your church in the coming year. You also need to pray that they will "stick."[3] They need to get plugged in to community and grow in the faith. After you pray about this, train your congregation in friendship evangelism and schedule outreach events on your annual calendar. When the body of Christ gets laser focused on making disciples, energy in the worship services will increase.

COMMUNITY SERVICE

Most of us in church leadership circles have dealt with mission statements, vision statements, and core values. What we typically have not thought through is how to describe all of this in a service theme.

I believe that thinking through the felt and real needs we are meeting in the local church will help turn attendees into advocates. Now, I can hear the critics saying, "Shouldn't the starting place be with the Word of God and the mission of Christ?" And the answer is yes. But what is the mission of Christ? The Great Commandment and the Great Commission are the things Christ has asked us to focus on. And the Great Commandment and the Great Commission have to do with loving and reaching people as well as loving God. If we are serious about getting out of the philosophy department and taking the Great Commission to the streets, we have to ask, "What will it look like to love this community?" and "What will it look like to make disciples on the mission field the Lord has entrusted to us?"

65

For instance, you might discover that there is a great need for a tutoring program in your community. If you were to reach out to children with a tutoring program and in the process share the Good News of Jesus Christ and the kingdom of God, you could really create a significant movement. This would then become a service theme. This would in time start to impact your worship services. Never underestimate the power of identifying the needs you can meet in your community.

CONCERTS

To this day, I am eternally grateful to Calvary Chapel of Colorado Springs for strategically using concerts to reach people for Christ. I was one who was reached. When I was a teenager, Alan Combs (my music teacher) and Todd Williams (my close friend, who was a drummer) invited me to one concert after another: Sweet Comfort Band, Leon Pattillo, the Second Chapter of Acts, and Bob Bennett. I would go because I was a musician. Half the time I went to these concerts, I was either drunk or on drugs. Yet the preaching of the gospel was consistent. And as a result, I eventually found myself compelled by the Spirit of God to go forward to the altar calls. I think I went forward to at least a dozen altar calls. Even though it would take a while for me to truly believe that I was born again, I attribute all of that going forward to the Spirit of God calling me by name. In time I was baptized, and that was the celebration that solidified the fact that Christ by his Spirit had caused me to be born again.

The point is, concerts can provide a wonderful context to create a culture of invitation. This is what we want to accomplish: getting our people to invite others to the church. Now, concerts are not a substitute for being witnesses and sharing the gospel in the community. They complete it. If someone is investigating Christianity because of your influence, you should be asking, "When are they going to connect with the rest of the body of Christ?" Christianity might be an individual experience for Americans, but that certainly was not the pattern in the New Testament. Connecting with the community of Christ was the norm. When a person came to faith, the whole household usually followed. Then they were connected with other followers of Jesus Christ. Concerts provide opportunities to do this very thing today.

SPECIAL MUSICAL ARTISTS

Similarly, musical artists can provide a special punch to your worship services. We have had special musical artists come in and lead worship with our worship team. Then they have led us in worship with some special music they have written or recorded.

I am referring to a couple of categories of musical artists here. First of all, there are special musical artists who are in your community or city. Usually what happens is that they are off on a particular week from the worship rotation in their home church and would be delighted to come in and do some special music in your church.

I think we ought to stop thinking of the other church or the mega church in town as the enemy. We need to get away from the scarcity mentality that thinks every other church is the competition and that there isn't enough to go around.[4] I believe we can do a much better job of networking our artists in our communities. Artists are more than thrilled to be asked if they would like to come into your church and lead worship. And if the worship pastor has the music charts ready to go for the band and other vocalists, guest artists can come in and just make some magic.

Secondly, there are well-known recording artists. The key to bringing in these artists is to make sure that their philosophy of ministry matches what you are trying to accomplish in your local setting. Make sure these artists complement your worship service and accomplish a purpose.

SPECIAL GUEST SPEAKERS

People like guest speakers to be consistent with the quality of the primary preacher. If you have a preaching team, demand that all of the preachers on this team have the gift of teaching. Also demand that they all have the same work ethic when it comes to improving the craft of preaching. If people are used to a culture where there are multiple teachers who are all good, this team-teaching culture is really beneficial for the church.

You should always ask guest speakers to speak about their areas of expertise. For example, if you are going to be doing a study on the Sermon on the Mount and you have a nearby college or seminary professor whose expertise is on the Sermon on the Mount, having him or her come in and teach a weekend, part of the series, or all of the series could be really great. If you are doing a series on marriage and you have a couple come in and share on the topic to kick off or wrap up the series and do a weekend seminar, this could really bless the worship service.

One caution: make sure the guest speaker will complement where you are going as a church. Experts are there to serve the local church, not the other way around. When the guest speaker leaves, you are still the pastor of your congregation. Guest speakers should be like a shot of adrenaline to your programming. They should never derail what you are trying to accomplish.

MESSAGE SERIES

By far the best way to use teaching for momentum is to carefully think through your message series. It is easy to underestimate the power of preaching a series. A series can be a rallying point every four to twelve weeks. When it comes to establishing a culture of invitation, a message series can provide great material for an invite card.

Now, there are different philosophies as to how to put a message series together. If you are targeting seekers, you will probably hit the issues that need to be addressed and find the appropriate texts to address those issues. If you are trying to teach doctrine, think through your systematic theology categories and then find the appropriate texts to teach. Even if you are a book-by-book preacher, you can quickly analyze what a book is all about and then give it a modern title that will sum up what that series is all about.

For example, as I am writing this, I am finishing up a series in 1 Peter. As I studied 1 Peter, I realized that this encouraging letter to persecuted Christians was basically saying, "Hang in there. You have been transformed, are being transformed, and will experience total transformation in the near future." As I pondered with our pastor of worship and arts what in society best describes a transformation process, we agreed that the television show *Extreme Makeover* was what fascinated a vast number of people. Therefore, I called the series on 1 Peter "Extreme Makeover: The Spiritual Edition."

As I preached this series, I shared that our culture looks at the outward appearance, but the Lord looks at the heart. I shared that our transformation is that we are becoming like Christ. I shared that in the same way there is bruising following plastic surgery, there is bruising in being a Christian; the Holy Spirit is cutting away everything that is hindering us from looking like Jesus.

Again, I do not think we have to choose between being culturally relevant or textually accurate. Why do we need to be binary when it comes to this issue? Why can't we be faithful to the text *and* relevant to the issues our people are struggling

69

with? This is the issue John R. W. Stott addressed when he spoke about living between two worlds. We must exegete the text, but we must also exegete our culture. As we strive to preach a message series, I believe we are forced to think about this issue. And I believe that as we do this with excellence, people will talk and say, "You've gotta be there." They will say, "The music is great, the people are friendly, and the teaching is really a blessing." God will begin to use us to reach out to our communities that so desperately need to hear the Good News of Jesus Christ and the kingdom of God.

I encourage you to have a solid theological orientation when it comes to worship service planning, but I also encourage you to have an entrepreneurial spirit. Try new and innovative initiatives that will give your people incentive to invite their friends to your church. Certainly focus on the quality, but also ponder the human needs you are addressing and then begin to tell your community about your church. We need to aggressively think of ways to connect with our community. We need to pray that our church would be like a magnet, drawing all who are looking for life in Christ. And then we need to pray that when they actually arrive, this is in fact what they will find. The Lord is ready to bring the city to our doorstep, but are we ready? As we would clean up our house before inviting someone over for dinner, we need to clean up the mediocrity we have settled for in the local church. Garden-variety worship is unacceptable. It is not what God wants from us. And it certainly is not what spiritually desperate people are longing for. People are longing for a taste of heaven. Go out of the way to have a hospitable spirit toward people looking for Jesus. When they encounter this kind of hospitable community, they will in turn say, "You've gotta be at this church." This is my prayer for your church and for mine. May God grant us life-giving churches!

six

OUTREACH MARKETING

As we continue with the issue of how to invite people to church so that they can encounter the living God, we need to consider outreach marketing. People either embrace marketing or reject the idea, thinking we are going to turn the church into a business. The reality is that every church is engaged in some level of marketing, starting with an ad in the phone book. If your church is listed in the phone book, you have already embraced the idea of marketing. If your church is associated with a radio ministry or publishing projects, you have embraced marketing regardless of all the hype of how marketing is secularizing our churches. When I say we need to consider "marketing," I am simply stating that we must get the message out that we are offering life in Christ Jesus and that our church exists in this particular community. In the same way that you would send out an invitation for a wedding, you must send out an invitation for your worship services. We must let others know about an event that will change their lives.

WORD OF MOUTH

Marketing starts with people, not with paper. If people become devoted followers and ministers of Jesus Christ, they will begin to reach out to others and invite them to a place where their family and friends can find life. The bottom line is that if people are not inviting others to your church, they are not that excited about what is happening.

People should be bragging about their churches like a grandfather brags about his grandchildren. A healthy grandparent will talk about his grandkids and pull out pictures to tell everyone all he can about how wonderful those kids are. In addition to pulling out the pictures, he will also weave stories about special moments, all the way down to the nuances of certain idiosyncrasies. That is normal.

Any time we are proud of something, we talk. Any time we experience something great, we talk. That's right! Human beings have a propensity for opening their mouths whenever they experience something great. If we see a really good movie, we tell others. If we hear a really wonderful song, we tell others.

Your best marketing is always going to be word of mouth. Before you try to do anything else, get your people talking about your church. Before you even begin to think about advertisement literature, think about your people. In the business world, the best marketing is a satisfied customer. In the church, the best marketing is a satisfied customer. If your people are not excited about your church, why should anyone else be? If the believers in your congregation are not bubbling up with the joy of the Lord, why would a person from your community who is struggling with major emotional issues want to come to your church? If the people currently attending your weekend services are not experiencing a taste of heaven, why would they invite others? People, your people, are the key to talking your church up in your community.

WEBSITE

The next checkpoint for marketing your church is your website. If I had written this chapter ten years ago, I would have said the phone book was your most important paid advertisement. These days, when an individual or family moves into your community, they will have already done a search on the Web to check out your church. Once they move into the community, they will check your website for directions to your church.

First of all, organize the most important information on your website. First things first! The order of priority for me would be as follows:

1. When are your weekend services?
2. How do you get to your church?
3. What kinds of children's and student ministries do you have?
4. What is your mission? What are your core values? What is your vision?
5. What does your worship and arts ministry look like?
6. What kind of adult ministries do you have?
7. What kind of missions program do you have?
8. What other kind of ministries do you have?
9. What is your doctrinal statement?
10. What is the history of your church and movement/denomination?
11. Who is on your staff? Who are the other contacts?
12. What does your weekly/monthly schedule look like?
13. What kind of links do you have on your site? (This reveals a lot about what influences your church.)
14. What other seminars/events do you host?

Your list might put these in a different order. All I have done is tried to think through the priorities of a first-time guest. The best way to gain an appreciation for a guest's perspective is to visit other churches when you are on vacation. My family has made this a habit on every vacation. Regardless of where we are, we always go to worship on the weekend and try to visit different churches to give us a fresh appreciation for the body of Christ. As a dad, there is a reason I put children's and student ministries third on my list. When we visit a church, we want to know details such as, "Where is the nursery? Do they have children's programming for kids during the worship services? Do we take our kids with us to worship?" You need to understand that I am not talking about philosophy of ministry at this point. I am simply asking, as a first-time guest, "What is expected of me? What am I supposed to do once I arrive at your church or campus? Where do I go? What do I do?" We in leadership in the local church really need to get this together if we are going to encourage people to worship. You should put this kind of information on your website.

ANSWERING MACHINES AND VOICE MAIL

If it is after office hours and someone calls your church, he or she should be able to access needed information quickly. Give options up front so that callers do not have to sit there and listen to a message that keeps on going.

You want to make sure you have an option for listening to service times and directions to your church. Do not forget to mention your website. Ask yourself, "If I were calling this number to find out about this church, what kind of information would I need to decide whether or not to visit the church?"

MARQUEE

You may ask, "Why on earth do we own a marquee? What is the purpose?" I ask these questions daily as I drive by churches.

It is obvious that many churches do not think their marquee is for marketing. It is obvious that many churches do not believe the purpose of their marquee is to give basic service times. This is obvious to me because of all the silly stuff I read on church marquees.

On the one hand, there are churches that use their marquees to preach. Most of the time, marquee preaching is churchy, like the guy on the street corner telling people where they are going to spend eternity. By the way, it usually is not the gospel if the gospel means Good News. Usually it is condemnatory and a turnoff.

On the other hand, some churches use their marquees for the slogan of the day. Yet the problem is that many of these slogans barely make sense to church people, much less to unchurched people. The plain fact is, the church is not advancing the gospel in the community when we make nonstrategic decisions. Do not junk up your marquee. Do not waste a communication opportunity. Use your marquee to provide needed service times. This is what your community wants and needs to know. They need to know when they can come to your church.

INTERNAL COMMUNICATION PIECES

The next marketing element for your church is internal communication pieces. Whatever you use, make sure they look sharp. If you use a trifold brochure, make sure all your ministries are represented. Also, do not underestimate the importance of having a brochure on your mission, core values, and vision. People want to know what you believe. They want to know where you are going. They care about the direction as much as the programming when looking for a new church.

Another type of internal communication that can say a lot about your church is hope literature. At Bethany we have a wall by our prayer room that is dedicated to providing literature that gives hope to those struggling with divorce, anger, eating disorders, financial or marriage problems, and perfectionism. These pieces of literature are uniform in that they are the same size and same design with different colors, pictures, and content. The reason this is important is that a lot of information centers and resource centers in the local church can get "junked up."

What do I mean by junked up? First of all, they are not well stocked. Secondly, the brochures are printed on different sizes of paper with different standards of quality. One brochure looks great, and another does not. This gives the overall impression that this ministry is not a priority. Do not let your information center or your resource center get cluttered. If you are starting off, utilize the wonderful resources from organizations like Focus on the Family (www.family. org) or Outreach Marketing (www.outreachmarketing.com). These are the two organizations we use because of the quality of their products. Outreach Marketing has some wonderful brochures for internal communication for ministries such as children's ministries, student ministries, worship, and arts. They provide the design, and you put in the ministry title and information. Focus on the Family has sought to minister to the needs people are struggling with at home and at work. Access their brochures. The investment you make here will have a good return.

EXTERNAL COMMUNICATION PIECES

Concerning communicating with your community, do not underestimate the power of external communication pieces. I believe that the most successful external communication pieces are invite cards. There are some important advantages to invite cards. First of all, you create a culture of invitation where your people take the initiative to invite others to their home church. They are the ones who hand out the cards. Again, this is promoting the word-of-mouth epidemic. Second, you are giving your community basic information: where your church is located (with a map on one side of the card), your service times, and the topic of the new series. This gives your community directional information as well as information about what your church is doing within its four walls.

Invite cards do not require postage stamps, making them an inexpensive way to advertise. If you are trying to reach the masses of your community, cards with postage stamps are questionable at best in terms of their effectiveness. People are going to be much more inclined to come to church if someone personally invites them. Furthermore, if a seeker comes to Christ, it is easier to do follow-up if he or she has been invited by someone in the church. And most importantly, you are training the congregation to take the initiative in building relationships with their friends and family members wherein the gospel will eventually be introduced.

If you want to do big community advertisements for special seasonal or cultural events, build relationships with the religious editors of your local newspaper. We are used to tossing junk mail, but we still read newspapers. Editors usually are more than willing to publish a story if it is well written and if there is a relationship between the editor and someone on your staff, preferably the senior pastor.

For example, if you are doing something special for Christmas or Easter, try to get a story published in the local newspaper. When a catastrophic event such as 9/11 or Columbine takes place, write a healing Christian response to that event. When movies like *The Passion of the Christ* are released, write a positive review. When books such as *The Purpose-Driven Life*, *The Prayer of Jabez*, or the Left Behind series are released, write a thoughtful editorial.

Something I learned from Leith Anderson, who connects with the local papers extremely well, is that when you are building relationships with local editors, be knowledgeable of the ethics that are involved. For example, you cannot buy lunch for the editor of a local newspaper. As weird as this may sound, investigate these issues prior to building a relationship. Find out what is permissible and what is not. The best way to do this is simply to admit ignorance and ask someone in the field.

ADDING MARKETING TO YOUR BUDGET

Make sure you do not forget to add marketing to your budget. Every little brochure adds up. Every little invite card begins to impact your outreach budget. Even something as seemingly insignificant as a yellow pages ad is actually quite expensive. Yet the payoff will be significant for having an attractive yellow pages ad, website, brochures, and invite cards. At some point, you need to decide whether or not doing things right is worth the financial cost to you. Although you pay on the front end, you will see the benefits when your community starts coming to your church.

I started off this chapter by saying that many churches have difficulty with the concept of marketing. People who go on a rant about marketing are usually inconsistent in word and deed. For example, everyone has a yellow pages ad. It is a given.

If you do not like the word *marketing*, call it something else, like *communication opportunity*. It does not matter what you call it, but you have got to do it. If you believe that your church has good news and if you believe that the Good News of Jesus Christ and the kingdom of God can change your community. Tell someone! This is the essence of the Good News. Be a town crier. Tell people that they *can* find hope.

Tell them *where* they can find it. If your motivation is to introduce people to Christ, then be creative. If your motivation is to colabor with Jesus when he says, "I will build my church, and the gates of Hades will not overcome it," then build the church in the power of the Spirit. Tell your community that your church offers hope.

In the Bible, gospel preaching was done in community. The local church exists to make a kingdom difference together. When an individual comes to Christ, what is next? The answer is that he or she needs to get plugged in to a local church. You cannot do Christianity alone. You can only live out the Christian life in Christian community.

Therefore, let us work together in the local church to tell people about Christ. Let us do everything possible to tell people how to get to our church, to communicate what a place of hope it is. Let us do everything we can to create a culture that is proud of the local church. Let us do everything we can to get people talking about the local church as though it were their favorite place in the whole world. This is what I mean by outreach marketing. This is a key variable in the complete worship service.

seven

PARKING, OUTSIDE SIGNAGE, AND ATTENDANTS

It is imperative for pastors, worship leaders, and the body of Christ to realize that a guest makes up his or her mind whether or not to return to your worship service before he or she ever hears the music or preaching. John Ortberg said, "I learn about the effectiveness of my ministry by watching people in the parking lot rather than in the pews."[1] If you are the owner of a fine restaurant, the atmosphere is just as important as the food. The same is true if you are inviting a guest over to your home. We typically work hard getting our homes cleaned for a special guest, but we tend to overlook this preparation when it comes to the local church. We need to make access to our facilities reasonable and enjoyable.

PARKING

We must do everything possible to reduce the headache factor when it comes to finding a parking spot. How many church growth books have you read that talk about the importance of adequate parking? Well, if you are like me, a ton of books. It keeps coming up over and over again. It is very important. It is so important that your church might be telling visitors that you are not interested in them if you are not dealing with this issue. Remember, if God is drawing people from your community to experience a taste of heaven, parking is essentially an issue of hospitality. If you want people to come to your church, you need to have a place for them to park their cars.

The worship experience starts when people pull into your property. If they have to wander all over the place before they can find a parking place, they will just move on. A couple of years ago, Susan and I and our kids visited a large church in Southern California.

When we arrived, about an hour early to get settled in, we could not find a parking space anywhere. Actually, I was quite surprised that the parking was as chaotic as it was. Not only were all the designated slots filled, but people were parked in front and in back of the designated spots. I thought to myself, *They're breaking all kinds of fire codes.* Since we wanted to go to church there, we eventually joined the chaos and parked our van in a place where my conscience was telling me, *You're going to get a ticket.* And yet that diabolical voice responded by saying, *If they are going to give you a ticket, then all these other people are going to get tickets too. Surely, they've received clearance from the police department.*

Once we got onto the campus, it took us forever to figure out where to take our kids. Our kids were ages eight, four, two, and one. At this church, that meant dropping them all off in different wings of the campus. After we dropped off the two youngest kids—that took a good half hour, with finding the place, signing them in, and all—I finally told my wife, "Forget this. Let's just take the older kids into the worship service with us." By the time the service started, I was stressed out

82

and in no mood to worship. It all started by not being able to find a parking place.

I told my wife that had I not been a Christian who wanted to visit this famous church, I would have gone out for lunch that day. Had I been a seeker trying to go to church, I would have given up. The effort was too frustrating. If you have room to expand your parking, expand it. Never underestimate the importance of your parking situation.

DESIGNATED GUEST PARKING

To contrast the previous story, I would like to tell you a positive parking lot story. On one of my family vacations, we decided to stay in Colorado. On the weekend, we came back into the Denver area and went to a very healthy evangelical church. I am actually going to tell you the name of the church because we had such a positive experience. It is Grace Chapel.

When we arrived, there was guest parking right by the children's center, which was on the way to the worship center. As soon as we got out of our car, there was an individual there who welcomed us and asked us if this was our first time at the church. We said yes. He saw that we had young children and asked us if we would like help dropping off the kids. We thought, *This guy is great, kind of like a personal guide.* We took him up on his offer. He helped us get the kids settled and then led us to the worship center. He showed us the information center and said he would be in that area if we needed any help. We thanked him right then as well as on our way back out.

Grace Chapel has placed their guest parking spaces in a strategic place. They also have greeters ready to help those who use those spaces. The greeters have been trained in what to do from that point on. The great thing was, they were helpful but not overbearing. You have to find that balance. If you have purchased a car recently, you know what I am talking about.

Some dealers have sales reps ready to attack you like sharks. Others have people who are there to help and ask you what you are looking for. They let you sell yourself instead of forcing their opinion and presence upon you. The same countenance needs to be present in your guest-care team.

Use parking strategically and also be aware of the phrases you use. "Visitor parking" says that you are expecting them to just visit. "Guest parking" is warmer and implies that they can always be your guest.

Remember, parents with small kids are thinking about dropping off their kids. In the two stories I have shared with you, you heard from a father who was either frustrated by or grateful for the experience that was extended to him. Realize that young families think about some very basic issues before they think about being blessed by the music or the message. They simply want to know where to park and where to drop off the kids. From the moment people drive into your parking lot, it should be obvious to them what to do and where to go. Provide clear information about where the children's wing is.

Parking for Seniors and Those with Disabilities

In addition to providing care for young families, make your facilities accessible to the elderly and disabled. You are saying you love senior adults and people with disabilities. You are saying you believe God wants older people and people with disabilities to have a taste of heaven. These parking spots should be right in front of your worship center or sanctuary. Senior adults and people with disabilities need to be able to get to the worship center with as little walking as possible and a minimum of stairs.

I did not realize how important this was until a couple of years ago when my dad had a heart valve replacement. It was critical prior to and after the operation that he not have too far to walk. The handicapped sign he hung from his rearview mirror was very helpful. And being with him when he went anywhere, whether it was a supermarket or a department store, made me realize just how important having this kind of parking is to the local church. When you consider that many of our seniors have gone through hip replacements, knee replacements, heart surgery, and a multitude of other procedures, you quickly realize how important parking is for an enjoyable worship experience.

PARKING ETIQUETTE

Correlated with parking for people with disabilities, seniors, and guests, it is important to train your leadership and ministry teams to be servants on Sunday mornings and park as far away as possible in order to leave the best spots for first-time guests. A related leadership issue arises when different groups go on retreats. If they take vans or buses, remind those going on the retreat to leave their cars in the farthest spaces to leave the nearer ones open for guests.

OUTSIDE SIGNAGE

As we continue to try to help people get settled into our church, it is important to have good outside signage. Let people know where the sanctuary is. Let them know where the offices are. At our church, the offices are far away from the sanctuary. During the middle of the week, the UPS person would always go to the sanctuary. Finally, our coordinator of church operations put out signage that indicated where the midweek entrances were for package drop-offs for the office.

We assume that people intuitively know where to go. We cannot do this. People do not know the layout of our facilities.

Make it clear. Now, you might be thinking, *I'm not a pastor of a mega church. Our church is pretty small. They'll figure it out.* Well, I say to you, if you can put a welcome mat on the front porch of your home, you can do the same for guests who come to your church. If people come into your home and ask, "Where's the restroom?" don't you think they might ask similar questions when they come to your church? Be hospitable. Help people out at every level.

What happens in the parking lot is the start of the worship experience. Give people a positive experience before they set foot in your sanctuary. Reach out to them with the kind of hospitality and forethought you would if Billy Graham were coming to your church. Plan the details as though the president of the United States and the first lady were visiting your services. The bottom line is that all of this is an attitude issue. When we expect something great to happen, we plan for it. Take some time to plan for something spectacular to happen this week at your church.

eight

DEVELOPING DYNAMIC GUEST CARE TEAMS AND SYSTEMS

Do not underestimate the importance of having a guest care center and guest care teams in place. Now, some of you might be thinking that I am talking "big church" language at this point. But nothing could be further from the truth. I am addressing an issue that small and medium-sized churches must begin to implement if they are going to improve their worship services. As I think about this topic, I cannot help but think of the reputation of Nordstrom. In the book *The Nordstrom Way: The Inside Story of America's #1 Customer Service Company*, Robert Spector and Patrick D. McCarthy share about some of the employees' heroics:

> A customer, who was about to catch a flight at Seattle-Tacoma Airport, inadvertently left her airline ticket at the counter in one of Nordstrom's women's apparel departments. Discovering the ticket, her Nordstrom sales associate immediately phoned the airline and asked the service representative if she could track down the customer at the airport and write her another ticket. No, she could not. So the Nordstrom salesperson jumped into a cab, rode out to the airport (at her own

expense), located the customer, and delivered the ticket herself. (Nordstrom later reimbursed her for the cab fare.)[1]

As I think about such stories from the business world, I wonder how we are doing in the local church. If a plane ticket was left in our church, would we do the same thing? Do we go out of our way to serve the people coming to our church? Do we really care about their needs? Do we really show them hospitality? There is a Polish proverb that says, "A guest sticks a nail in the wall even if he stays but one night." Is this how we make our guests feel? Do we make them feel at home? As we think about our guest care systems, we need to reflect on how people coming to our churches perceive our care and concern for them.

FIND AMIABLE PEOPLE

The starting place for developing dynamic guest care teams and systems is to find people who are warm, loving, kind, and friendly. Trust me, it is an absolute disaster to try to take sour, grouchy people and train them to put on a smile. That is not how you find good greeters. Find people who are amiable and helpful and who take initiative. Find people who are magnetic. Big people are those who make us feel bigger when we are around them.[2]

There is a fine line between finding people who are helpful and avoiding overly zealous people who smother guests. Guests want to use a certain amount of anonymity when checking out a new situation. Avoid placing overeager people in your key greeter roles.

Part of amiability is the ability to ask a few key questions and then to stop talking. I have visited a few churches where the greeters/hosts made you feel like you were the only visitor they had had in a decade. Yikes! They just could not stop talking about all the stuff at their church.

I once visited a church where I went up to the information center to glance at their brochures. I wanted to get an idea of the layout of some of their publications. The person running the guest center just could not stop talking. She did not once ask me a question. She was like the Energizer Bunny: she just kept going and going and going. Friend, believe me, this is a turnoff to a guest. Have your information hosts simply ask, "Do you have any questions about any of our ministries?" and then let the guest determine whether the conversation will go any further. George Barna in his book *User Friendly Churches* states:

> Anonymity for visitors was not perceived to be negative by the leaders of growing churches. They recognized that many people visit a church with trepidation, and with a desire to take things slowly. These cautious visitors often prefer to remain part of the woodwork for awhile, acting as participant-observers, unobtrusive and unfettered. The leaders of these churches also believed that the members of the congregation could be relied upon to do what was reasonable and necessary to make the visitor feel welcomed, but not cornered.[3]

The greeter/host should simply provide information. Therefore, greeters/hosts should also work on clarity and brevity. The clearer the directions and information, the more the guest will appreciate it. The more elongated information becomes, the more confusing it becomes. Again, brevity is linked with clarity. If guests ask a simple question, they should receive a simple answer. Do not answer questions they are not asking.

GREETERS SHOULD BOTH STAND OUT AND BLEND IN

First of all, greeters should stand out. In other words, you should place your greeters in key locations. If you are a guest, you should be greeted as soon as possible. It is a shame to make your way through a church and not be greeted. Singer John Charles Thomas, at age sixty-six, wrote to syndicated columnist Abigail Van Buren, "I am presently completing the second year of a three-year survey on the hospitality or lack of it in churches. To date, of the 195 churches I have visited, I was spoken to in only one by someone other than an official greeter and that was to ask me to move my feet."[4]

When I was a student at Fuller Seminary, I would go to Saddleback Community Church. There were always people there to welcome me as soon as I got out of my car. I went to Saddleback when they were meeting in big tents, and I kept seeing the Saddleback campus grow every time I went back there. The buildings started going up. Obviously, God's hand of blessing has been on that church. Yet one of the variables of their growth is how they use their greeters in the parking area.

Greeters should also be in the key entrance areas welcoming people. If you are a guest, you should be greeted by at least three people before you end up in the worship center. Again, the complete worship service starts before you ever get into the sanctuary. Make guests feel welcome. Remember, this is an issue of hospitality. Make them feel at home, and let them have some breathing room to check things out at their own pace.

BEYOND HANDING OUT PAPER

As we begin to discuss the role of ushers, we must ask, "What is the difference between having a person hand you a bulletin and just picking up a bulletin on your way into a service?" And the answer is that when a person hands you a bulletin, he or she should make human contact. Many ushers think the only exchange is the exchange of paper. No, the exchange is the warm welcome of kind words and a smile to go with the words.

Ushers need to see their role as devoted ministers of Jesus Christ. They need to realize that the smile they offer someone might be the only smile that guest or regular attendee will receive all week long. People are pretty discouraged. People are looking for hope. People are looking for love. And if your ushers reach out and communicate love and caring to your guests and regular attendees, your congregation will comment on how warm and friendly your church is.

Ushers also need to know what to do if your services are filling up. How do they help a guest find seating in a packed sanctuary? What are they looking for? Ushers need to be helpful in these situations and not just allow guests to wander around frustrated.

Ushers must also be able to answer questions the greeter was not asked, such as "Where is the nursery?" or "Do you have a cry room?" And the most important question of all: "Where are the restrooms?" Ushers should not be fumbling around on questions like this. They need to know the basic layout of the facilities. They need to be able to guide people when they ask for help. They need to personally escort someone with a question to the answer instead of just giving him or her verbal information. Do not point; show. It is a sign of courtesy to just go with the person to the nursery. It is an act of love and of service to tell that guest, "Follow me, and I'll just take you there." These little touches can make or break a church just like they can make or break a business.

Ushers must also be trained for emergencies. Remember that it is always possible for a fire alarm to go off. If there is an emergency, your people need to know what to do. What happens if someone has an epileptic seizure? What happens if someone has a heart attack? Do ushers know how to respond?

About seven years ago, we had a very interesting situation happen in a worship service at Bethany. We had a couple of "street prophets" come in and hijack our worship service. At the time, I was the worship leader at Bethany. Right in the middle of our pastor's sermon, these street prophets came in and gave a three-minute speech on how we needed to take care of the poor. Because our pastor was such a gracious man, he just let this happen. Maybe he was also trying to hear if the Lord was in their message. I think, if we were honest, none of us knew quite what to do. We had never planned for something like this. Our pastor thanked them and then said a brief prayer after they left that God would help us make sense of what they had said.

My difficulty with this whole situation had to do with the fact that the words of the message were right on but the timing was way off. I mentioned that it felt like they hijacked our worship service, because their entrance was so disorderly. My interpretation of 1 Corinthians 14 is that this kind of thing should be done in order. What do your ushers do in this kind of situation? If the pastor gives the appropriate look to the lead usher, will something happen? Are the ushers ready to respond to these kinds of situations?

Hopefully, you do not hear me encouraging ushers to be bouncers. They just need to know how to respond to situations like this in love. They need to be decisive and move quickly. They need to make the appropriate decisions and be people of action. You need to have someone who has CPR and first aid training. Safety must fit into your core values.

You should also find ushers and greeters who match your community. In other words, do not reserve ushering for just one segment of your constituency. Get some students in the mix. Get some young couples serving in this role. Be more egalitarian. Why do we have only men ushering or greeting in many of our evangelical churches? Who wrote the unspoken rule that eliminates students from serving? Why do we have such a problem with children serving in these roles? We do ourselves a great disservice by underestimating the potential of the upcoming generations. At the same time, keep your seniors involved.

And to all the senior pastors and worship pastors reading this, it is up to us to give leadership in this area. It is up to us to demand a little more in this area. It is up to us to inspire our lead ushers to train, schedule, and make things happen. We simply cannot wait around for better days. We must create the future by what we do in the present. These issues are simply too important to neglect.

In the book *Be Our Guest: Perfecting the Art of Customer Service*, the Disney Institute has a wonderful chart of expectations they have of their cast members (employees). This chart should be applied to greeters, ushers, and all involved with guest care ministry:

Walt Disney World Guidelines for Guest Service

Make Eye Contact and Smile!
• Start and end every Guest contact and communication with direct eye contact and a sincere smile.

Greet and Welcome Each and Every Guest
• Extend the appropriate greeting to every Guest with whom you come into contact.

"Good morning/afternoon/evening!"

"Welcome!" "Have a good day."

"May I help you?"

• Make Guests feel welcome by providing a special differentiated greeting in each area.

Seek Out Guest Contact
• It is the responsibility of every Cast Member to seek out Guests who need help or assistance.

Listen to Guests' needs

Answer questions

Offer assistance (For example: Taking family photographs)

Provide Immediate Service Recovery
• It is the responsibility of all Cast Members to attempt, to the best of their abilities, to immediately resolve a Guest service failure before it becomes a Guest service problem.

- Always find the answer for the Guest and/or find another Cast Member who can help the Guest. . . .

Thank Each and Every Guest

- Extend every Guest a sincere thank-you at the conclusion of every transaction.[5]

I would also emphasize: Be sincere. Be authentic. The key is not to treat people as a means to something else. Be present and appreciate their company. "The opposite of talking is not listening. The opposite of talking is waiting."[6] Enjoy the moment with other people.

GUEST CARE CENTERS

Many times when we are thinking about putting a guest care center together, we are thinking simply about representing our ministries. We already talked about the need to have internal communication pieces, but I would like to take a moment and take this to the next level.

If we want to tell people how to get involved, we need to let them know not only how we can serve them but also how they can serve the church and their community. We need to begin to expect people to serve according to their giftedness. We then need to provide the necessary training.

Do you have a brochure that tells people how to get involved now that they have come to your worship service? Do you have a communication piece that lets them know what to do next? What kind of process do you have to take people to the next level? How do you connect first-time guests into your community?

At Bethany we put on the back of the bulletin a process simply called "Get Connected." We use the symbol of an electrical outlet. We walk people through a four-step process that encourages them to get involved at the next level. In step one, we encourage them to fill out the communication card attached to the bulletin and let us know how we can serve them and to indicate what concerns and interests they have. In step two, we encourage them to stop by the information center and check out the ministry brochures and to log on to our website. In step three, we encourage them to get a cup of coffee at the café and ask them to attend one of our adult Bible fellowships the following Sunday. And in step four, we ask them to sign up for the Discovering Bethany class we offer once a month on Sundays from 4:00 to 8:00. We also offer a series of classes designed to get people integrated into the church community. You must have some kind of process to move people from window shoppers to servants of Christ. You need to tell people how to move from being guests to being involved in community to being discipled to discipling others. Do not simply provide pamphlets on programming. Emphasize process.

DEVELOPING A HOSPITABLE SPIRIT

Along with having a process-centered guest care center, you should also create a warm atmosphere by providing coffee, tea, and pastries. In many of our churches, this happens in a Sunday school or classroom context. But we need to move this hospitality into the foyer and outside before people ever get to a worship service.

If I am going to invite people over to my home, the first thing I will do, after taking their jackets, is to offer them a cup of coffee or something to drink. This same mind-set should permeate our churches. We should have a hospitable spirit. If we are showing people what heaven will be like, hospitality is imperative. God is drawing people from all over the world to one day celebrate a meal in his presence. This glorious hope must be foreshadowed this weekend in our churches. For me, the spirit of hospitality is captured in the movie *My Big Fat Greek Wedding*.

Toula Portokalos . . . is the daughter of a restaurateur who owns Dancing Zorba's restaurant in Chicago. . . .Toula meets Ian Miller . . . and they immediately hit it off. As the relationship develops, Toula becomes increasingly concerned that because Ian is not Greek, her parents will not approve of the relationship. . . . Even though they gradually consent to their daughter's choice, the family insists that Ian adopt their Greek culture and faith.

When Ian's parents (a wealthy couple without any extended family) accept a dinner invitation at Toula's parents' home, they are not prepared for what they experience. . . . They are greeted on the front lawn by nearly 100 people—the entire Portokalos clan. Amid the dozens of cousins, aunts and uncles (most of whom are named "Nick"), there is a goat hanging on a spit over an open fire.

Toula's father, Gus, addresses the Millers above the boisterous crowd. He smiles broadly and says, "Welcome to my home!" Toula's mother approaches the bewildered couple and gives them the traditional hug and kiss on the cheek. . . . Gus and his extended family then warmly welcome the Millers inside the home for an evening of Greek-style feasting and hospitality.[7]

There is quite a bit of humor concerning the ethnicity of hospitality in *My Big Fat Greek Wedding*. Yet I believe that our churches should have the same hospitable spirit represented by the Portokalos family. People are really looking for community. People are looking to be accepted. They are looking for a place that extends warmth and kindness. They are looking for a place to experience feasting and hospitality. This is a deep longing in every human heart. "Share with God's people who are in need. Practice hospitality" (Rom. 12:13).

CAFÉS ENHANCE COMMUNITY

The best way to enhance community is to design a café, even if you have just a little corner providing a couple of choices of coffee and some cookies. This kind of atmosphere is wonderful. Now, if you can add some round tables with some chairs and create your own little café, this is even better.

This is not just a European cultural issue anymore. Ever since Starbucks took over the world, people are accustomed to going into designated areas in which they can just hang out. Having a café promotes community. People will spend time talking with other people after a service if they have someplace they can sit down and have a cup of coffee.

What I find interesting is that churches are jumping on the coffee cart idea and providing lattes, cappuccinos, and a host of other drinks. But they typically do not provide anywhere to sit down and hang out. You need not only the coffee but also somewhere to rest and start up a great conversation. This type of café requires a team with a servant attitude to stay, serve, and create this atmosphere. We want not only a hospitable atmosphere but also an opportunity to build community. Invest in an area in your church where you can have some round tables, chairs, and décor that gives the feel of a French café. Go the extra mile by providing a special atmosphere.

Most importantly, extend your hospitality beyond your comfort zone. Reach out to people who tend to get overlooked. We have people-blindness in our churches. We need to see people as Jesus sees people. This reminds me of a story I recently heard:

> In 1970, when I was about 15, we and some other guests were invited . . . to dinner. I recall these other two guests being very kind women: an elderly, somewhat crippled lady and her personal assistant, an African-American lady named Addie.
>
> When it was time for dinner, the long table was filled with food. We said grace and began to indulge. About halfway through the meal, I noticed someone was missing. It was Addie. I did not think much of it at the time; I assumed she was not feeling well.

On the way home that night I asked my mom what had happened to Addie. My mother told me to call her "Miss Addie," and then told me what had happened. Her answer shocked me. Our hostess's sister, who had cooked our meal, had grown up with the tradition that black and white people did not eat together at the same table. And so Miss Addie had been told to eat by herself in a separate room. Neither my mother nor I could believe this had happened in this home that we had come to love and respect, and we both hurt for Miss Addie.[8]

This kind of behavior is unacceptable. We are to show hospitality to those who get neglected in our society and in our culture. The question for us is, who are the Miss Addies in our churches? Who are the Miss Addies in our communities? Who is missing from our dinner tables? May we not only make a place for the Miss Addies but also make a special meal. Remember, this is exactly what the Father is doing. He is preparing a meal for the outcast and the neglected in our society. He is preparing a wedding banquet where the Miss Addies will be. Therefore, when we reach out to the marginalized in society, Jesus will be smiling down on us.

Concluding Thoughts

Never underestimate the potential of offering quality hospitality. When greeters, ushers, and hosts are at their best, people will remember the extra care you took to provide that special environment. Taking some time to create hospitality in your own context will prepare hearts for worship as well as solidify a wonderful experience following worship for your church.

If for some reason you have a difficult time envisioning what hospitality looks like, simply visit some other churches in your area that are doing hospitality well. Then go to a

Starbucks and do more than place an order. Have a seat and ask yourself why this kind of atmosphere is so important to people. Go to stores like Nordstrom and ask, "Why do they have the reputation for customer service that they do?" Go to a neighborhood pancake house and evaluate their friendly service. Do not go alone, but go with your key leadership team. Use these opportunities as inquisitive field trips for your staff. Then ask, "How can we go the extra mile in providing a hospitable atmosphere in the local church?" This will make all the difference in creating the complete worship service, which, as you have already discovered, means more than music and preaching. It is the whole experience in the same way that Disneyland is more than the rides. It is the music, the customer service, the cleanliness of the park, and other variables that the cast (employees) execute so that people will have the best experience possible.

PART THREE

EXPERIENCING
A TASTE OF HEAVEN

nine

THE WORSHIP CENTER

In this chapter, we will address the sensory experiences people should have when they enter the worship center or sanctuary. This variable is important because it will either enhance or distract from our focus on Christ. First-time guests and returning members will notice the visual details that enhance worship services. In their book *The Sacred Romance: Drawing Closer to the Heart of God*, Brent Curtis and John Eldredge write:

> A friend of mine is a missionary to Muslims in Senegal. He tells me that after conversion, Muslims will often notice flowers for the first time. Prior to salvation, Muslims in that arid country live a very utilitarian existence. Things are valued only for what they can do. Their houses are dull and drab; trees are only appreciated if they are fruit trees; if they have a function. It is as if the Muslims have lived without beauty for their whole lives and now, having their souls released from bondage, they are freed into the pleasures of God's creative heart. I'm struck by the parallels to modern fundamentalism. Their hatred of pleasure is not a sign of their godliness; quite the opposite. The redeemed heart hungers for beauty.[1]

When people come to our worship services, we want to give them a taste of heaven. And heaven, I believe, is going to be a beautiful place. Let us help people not only experience the life Jesus came to give but also see the beauty of living in the kingdom of God.

LIGHTING

Do not underestimate the importance of lighting, whether bright, dim, or dark. Consideration of lighting in the sanctuary and on the platform is absolutely imperative.

In my previous book, *The Complete Worship Leader*, I talked quite a bit about the importance of *seeing* the body of Christ. Worship is something we do not just as individuals but with the rest of the body of Christ. It is critical that we are reminded that worship is something we do with the saints.

I am not implying that the lighting has to be as bright as the sun in your worship services. As a matter of fact, there are some services in which you want it a bit dimmer. There might even be some services that you do in complete darkness. Last Advent I preached a message about the people living in darkness seeing a great light. I preached the first ten minutes in complete darkness. Then as I talked about the Light coming into the world, we began to systematically light the candles in the sanctuary that provided the reminder that Christ is the Light of the World and that his light lives through his followers. The issue of what we did, or in this case did not do, with lighting, made this service.

Thoughtfully consider how to use light. If you are doing an upbeat celebration song, fill the sanctuary or worship center with lots of light. Celebration should be bright as well as exciting and fast. Use your lighting to communicate the mood you want to produce. Natural light is incredibly effective for special services like Easter. People like to see light on Easter Sunday morning. If you have lots of natural light through the windows in your sanctuary, use this when appropriate to create a mood of celebration.

For your communion services, dim the lighting, use some candles, and create that special atmosphere. When you dim the lighting, you create a more reflective mood. Again, realize that what you do with lighting can create the complete worship service. People are not coming to worship with only their auditory sense turned on. They are coming into the sanctuary in which what we do with lighting can either promote or detract from worship.

It is also worth noting that if you are asking for response—if you desire an atmosphere of transparency in which people come forward for prayer or other such responses—what you do with lighting will either encourage or discourage response. Now, this might sound manipulative, but the lighting creates the mood for a certain response. We want people to worship, and creating a certain atmosphere is not manipulative but intentional and conducive to worship. We want to create atmospheres that promote a response from God's people and from those whom God is drawing unto himself.

When I was a director for Continental Singers, we had a part in our program in which we would preach the gospel and ask for response. In those concerts, our spotlight technician would do something very simple. Along with the other technicians, he would create an atmosphere for people to respond to the gospel. The lighting tech would dim the lights, and the spotlight tech would aim the spotlight at the ceiling of the venue in which we were ministering. Then he would open the circumference of the circle of the spotlight. This created enough light to see people raise their hands. We, the Continentals, would then come off the risers and go and minister to those who lifted their hands. Believe me, after thousands of concerts, I saw thousands of people receive Christ in this kind of atmosphere.

The emotional aspect of this is that people want to make a decision but have never stepped in front of a crowd in a fully lit venue. I can hear the critics say, "If they can't come forward in front of the church, how will they be able to stand in the world?" When people are baptized, they are publicly declaring their faith in Jesus Christ before their family and friends. In our evangelical culture of come-forward invitations, baptism is almost anticlimactic. Now, please understand me, if come-forward invitations work in your context, by all means, do that. But if you are like most other churches where you ask for people to come forward and keep asking and keep asking and find no response, reconsider both how you are asking and what you are doing with lighting.

I believe that the dimmer the atmosphere, the more transparent people are. This sounds weird. It sounds like a paradox. But in fact, it is true. Therefore, always consider how you are using lighting to promote worship. Always consider how to improve your use of lighting to solicit response. Give someone the responsibility of working with your lighting. You may currently have a sound tech and a PowerPoint person. Now you need a lighting person. Invest in backlighting. Maybe you just need dimmer controls for the house lighting in your sanctuary. Lighting helps to focus people. Lighting should change with the transition from music to drama to sermon to response. People will focus their attention wherever the light is focused. Whatever your circumstance, assess the importance of lighting.

I am not saying that lighting is a substitute for the work of the Spirit of God. No one can come to Christ unless the Father draws them, and no one can be born again unless the Spirit of God regenerates. Lighting will never substitute for the preaching of the gospel. What I am saying is that we have made Christianity so religious that sharing the Good News in a nonthreatening environment is often overlooked. Take time to study the places in which our Lord did ministry. Many of these locations were not even religious settings. Atmosphere is very significant for creating a place for listening, learning, discussion, and spiritual conversation to effectively transpire.

Now, one last beef I have is, why is it that during the Advent season, every mall is all lit up, the businesses in town have beautiful lights, and the local churches are dark? This struck me one Advent season, and I declared that enough was enough. I declared war on the dark church during a season of light. I mandated that we must have Christmas lights not just inside our church but on the outside of the church as well. Our community needs to see that the church is the ultimate place of celebration during the season of joy. Now, this does not mean that we should be like Chevy Chase's character in the movie *Christmas Vacation*. We do not need to blind our communities. But I do think we should have some very attractive lights on the outside of our churches during the Advent season.

COLOR

How do you move from blah to wow? Well, your next action step for engaging the worshiper coming to your church is to ask, "How do we use color to communicate what we need to communicate today?" It starts by asking about the overall color scheme of your church. First, there is the external color scheme of the church. Is the outside paint job on your facilities attractive or distractive? Is the paint new or old? What kind of maintenance plan do you have for keeping the paint on the outside of the church fresh and clean? Never underestimate the impact of the external color scheme or quality of the facilities.

As you walk into your church, does the color on the walls and the ceiling complement the carpeting? Who made the decisions for your color scheme? It seems that our sisters and brothers who have an eye for color schemes should be the ones making decisions about color. Get your artists involved.

There seem to be two trends in the local church. On the one hand, there are churches with uncoordinated application of color. The churches in this situation seem to be the ones where every free space is taped with posters advertising every event on the calendar. This hinders preparation for worship.

On the other hand, you have churches that have become conscientious about the lack of coordination, and someone has taken the appropriate steps to set things straight. Yet these churches, although clean and attractive, lack artistic touch. They have sterile atmospheres. Our church just went from the disorganized to the sterile church. We have been working over the last two years to achieve a balance by adding more color and artistic touch to our facilities.

One of the ideas we have implemented is the stenciling of key Scripture verses on the walls of our foyer. For example, right before you go into our sanctuary, you see, "Better is one day in your courts than a thousand anywhere else." As you go to our café, you see, "Taste and see that the Lord is good." As you go to our prayer room (the fireside room), you see, "Ask, seek, and knock and it shall be given unto you." This stenciling adds a little color and is done in a way that gives our foyer a home environment.

In your sanctuary, use backlighting with colored gels to create additional moods. Shine a backlight with a red gel on your cross. Work with your backlighting by putting in the basic color gels to give you a wide variety of potential for mixing. Do not underestimate the power of what you do with color in your lighting, in your painting, in your carpeting. Color communicates so much: conservative, celebratory, legalistic, multicultural, sad, joyful, reflective, transcendent, immanent. The question you must ask is, what do we want to communicate?

CANDLES

A key element of postmodern culture is ancient-future worship—the combination of elements from the early church and technological advancements. Candles provide a reflective element. I am an evangelical who grew up Catholic. What I appreciated most about growing up Catholic was the atmosphere of the church. I never remember getting dropped off in the children's wing. The parish my family attended expected the whole family to worship together.

As a kid, I had no idea what was going on half of the time in the service. All I knew was that I was to make the sign of the cross after I dipped my finger in the holy water upon entering the sanctuary. When I went to my aisle, I would do a little kneel and make the sign of the cross. Then at certain points in the liturgy I would stand, kneel, or sit. I remember the Apostles' Creed, the Lord's Prayer, and the Hail Mary. Beyond these kinds of logistics, the things I remember most vividly are the stained glass, the stations of the cross, and most importantly, the candles.

I am aware that in some traditions, including some Catholic parishes, candles can be used for religious purposes. This goes beyond the aesthetic— for example, lighting a candle for a person for whom you are praying or lighting a candle for a deceased relative or friend and saying a prayer. It is not for these purposes that I encourage you to use candles. Rather, I am advocating the use of candles for creating reflective atmospheres. In our fast-paced culture, we need to slow down and reflect more frequently. We are passing up more than we are catching up to. Life is a mystery to be explored, not a problem to be solved. We have to get off the activity treadmill if we are ever going to hear the Spirit whisper to us.

In the evangelical context, let me simply ask you to reflect on your last Christmas Eve candlelight service. Hopefully, it was a positive experience. My guess is that it was a very meaningful service. Perhaps you turned off all the lights and talked about the world being in darkness. You lit that first candle and talked about Christ coming into this world, and one by one, you lit all the candles, a powerful visual of what Christ is doing in this world.

If that was a powerful moment for your worshipers, do not wait for Christmas Eve to use candles. Use candles on a regular basis in your worship services. Have you ever noticed how many specialty candle stores there are in the malls? That is because people like candles in their homes. They are soothing. They promote reflection. They are comforting. They are warm. Do you want these kinds of responses in your worship services? Then use candles.

This can be overdone. Do not light a thousand votives in your sanctuary. It gives the connotation that you are remembering the dead (although that would be appropriate if you have a memorial service and remembering the dead is your intention). Otherwise, you want to promote life. You want to promote a transcendent atmosphere for those who are weary. You want to promote a comforting atmosphere for the hurting. Again, I hope you do not hear me promoting some kind of weird, freaky spirituality. Our message is Christ. Our text is the inspired Word of God. Our mission is to make disciples. I am simply saying that our culture is disillusioned with secularism and is longing for transcendent worship services. If you do not provide transcendent worship with the gospel, your community will provide alternative attractive physical atmospheres with no gospel.

This issue is very significant as we consider ministering to a postmodern generation. They are looking for something that is otherworldly (my base definition of *transcendent*). I was teaching with Robert Webber and Michael Card at Andrews University earlier this year. Robert Webber mentioned that he is experiencing more and more students who are longing to celebrate the Lord's Supper and are looking for transcendent atmospheres. They are weary of everything else. They long for something special when they come to church. The use of candles can be very significant in creating these kinds of worship atmospheres.

PLANTS

Plants communicate life. Yet there are some extreme ways to use plants. The first extreme is churches with plastic plants all over the platform. You walk into these sanctuaries, and you could swear that you just entered the Amazon. It is overdone. It is too much. The only thing missing is the boat, animals, and jokes to make it a Disney jungle cruise. Be careful with this. Recruit an interior designer to safeguard how many plants are used.

The second extreme is real-plant churches whose plants are withered and dying. Yet because the investment was so costly, they remain in the sanctuary. This typically happens after Christmas, Palm Sunday, or Easter. The poinsettias, palm branches, and Easter lilies must be removed just like the Christmas tree after Christmas.

What we need are live plants when possible, plastic plants that do not look like plastic plants, and someone with a green thumb. Perhaps this "someone" could care for the plants in the middle of the week. We are blessed at Bethany in that our pastor emeritus, John Rynders, loves plants. He is the someone with the green thumb who puts the plants in locations where they get the necessary sunlight in the middle of the week. He waters these plants. He takes care of them in the same way he pastors people. When people come in, they see plants that are vigorous and full of life. The plants communicate that this is a church that promotes life.

111

Spend some money and get some attractive plants and place them around your foyer and certainly on the platform. This will promote a sense of life. It will communicate that your church is a church that is alive. It will provide a pleasant aesthetic quality that needs to be in the local church.

FLOWERS

Nice flower arrangements can enhance your worship services. I never realized this until our worship pastor put a line item under his worship and arts budget for flowers. Of course, I have experienced Easter lilies in the past, but flowers on a regular basis? Yes. Absolutely, yes. Flowers communicate so many things, but most importantly, they provide a lovely atmosphere.

Mother's Day is a perfect example of when to use flowers. Beautiful flowers portray the beauty of a mother's love and of God's love. Also, during the month of February, display red roses in beautiful arrangements in your sanctuary. Then give them to the women after the services. Encourage the men to come up and get roses for their wives. Make these roses available in your foyer as well. If you have a café, put roses on the tables.

At Bethany, we have also used roses for communion services. We had rose petals on the ground just in front of the communion stations. When people came forward for communion, they were singing, "Like a rose, trampled on the ground." This was a powerful reminder of how our precious Lord was mistreated so that we might have life.

Fresh-cut flowers should be arranged and displayed to enhance the worship experience. You obviously do not want the feel of a mortuary. Therefore, the arrangements should complement the color scheme, the thematic material of the service, and the mood of the service. With the combination

112

of lighting and arrangement of plants, the addition of flowers can add so much to the ambiance in the sanctuary. If you do not have an eye for flower arrangements, have someone join your team who does, and encourage him or her to make the sanctuary look beautiful.

Once again, there are budget issues. I realize that not all of you will be able to sustain regular flower arrangements in your annual budget. What I want to communicate is that whatever you can afford to do in this area will make a difference in creating a lovely atmosphere for your weekend services.

PLATFORM ARRANGEMENT

If your platform is chaotic, it will impact your emotional mood during the service. I have seen some church platforms that look like someone is making a bomb. Cables and cords are going everywhere. It is always amazing to me that the artists on these platforms do not end up tripping on the cords and breaking their necks.

It is imperative to organize cables on the platform. If the platform is an eyesore, it will subconsciously impact worship. Believe me, beauty is directly correlated with order. I encourage you to go back and read *The Complete Worship Leader* on this topic. I spend time in that book talking about the importance of order in the section entitled "Becoming an Artist."

Correlated with the issue of cables is the issue of microphone cords. Go wireless or clean up your microphone cords. It costs a little to invest in a wireless system, but the payoff is huge. The look is so much more professional. At our church, our worship pastor made this transition about a year ago, and I kick myself for not doing it earlier. The look is so much more professional. We want to eliminate anything that distracts from worship.

One last consideration for your platform is the issue of props and overall arrangement. The best way to address this issue is to have someone on your creative arts team who is thinking about the look of the platform on a weekly basis. This person can focus on how to use fabric, tapestry, and the rest of the visual arts.

If in your preaching you are using any kind of visual aids or props (I hope you are), you need to think about not only what kind of prop to use but also where on the platform it should go. These details should not be an afterthought. They should be rehearsed just like the music.

The overall arrangement of the platform needs to be co-ordinated. Someone needs to be thinking about the best place, acoustically and aesthetically, to put the drummer, the pianist, and the rest of the band. The arrangement of plants needs to go with the overall scheme of everything else that is going on. The overall look should be just as coordinated as the musical arrangements of the worship set you are doing. It is about the small details: balance, positioning (what is pleasing and comforting to the eye), sight lines, and so on. This extra thought is what makes the complete worship service.

POWERPOINT

First and foremost, your PowerPoint slides need to be read-able. It is one thing to put a presentation on your computer; it is another to test it in the sanctuary. Readability of the words needs to be the priority. Typically, this means you will be able to put only one element of a song on each slide. For example, you will have to put verse one, chorus, verse two, chorus, and bridge all on separate slides. If you try to put the whole song on one slide, the words will be too small to read. You have to check and evaluate these kinds of details.

The other issue you want to pay close attention to is the color of the text in contrast with the color of the background. The colors have to be readable. You have to test-run this on your projection system. What appears on your computer screen might not look the same on the projection system. It is not that your projection system will project different images or colors than what is on your computer (if that is happening, you have bigger problems), but the quality of the projection of your color scheme might not come off as you had hoped, and you cannot know this by simply looking at your computer screen.

It is also important to have a similar font for each song. If the font changes with each song, it is distracting. Having the same easy-to-read font in a color that is consistent throughout the PowerPoint presentation is very important. Test-run all of these elements!

Although the words must be a priority, use some creativity in your presentations. Bring in the arts here as well. The key is mood. Do not distort the mood with images that are too busy or too convoluted. What you use on the background needs to reflect the text and the mood you want to create.

With the text on PowerPoint, try some new entrances and exits. If you keep it the same way every week, it becomes too predictable. There are so many options to choose from. Just make sure that the entrances and exits of the text complement the mood you are trying to create. If you are trying to communicate a very serious point, and the text scrolls in like a party, it will conflict with what you are trying to communicate. Also, do not forget to have someone proofread the text. Misspelled words in choruses and preaching presentations appear too frequently in all our churches.

DRESS CODE?

My experience is that it is easy to be prideful about dressing down as much as about dressing up. I was a part of a movement for a decade that was really critical of people dressing up to come to church. We liked being the worst-dressed crowd in town. We prided ourselves on dressing down. This is what it meant for us to be "authentic."

If you are in a culture where people tend to dress down and this is part of your church culture, dressing up can be a distraction. On the other hand, if you are in a church culture where people dress up and you show up looking like John the Baptist, you will stand out and probably be a distraction. The key is not to draw attention to yourself but to allow the attention to be drawn to the Lord. People can actually turn away from church if the dress code does not match the community ethnography.

A few years ago an elderly couple at Bethany gave me one of the best gifts I have ever received. I always wore a coat and tie when I preached simply because I thought it was more professional. Yet, because I perspire like crazy when I preach, I was finishing the worship services soaking wet. This elderly couple said, "Pastor Kevin, you know you don't have to wear a coat and tie here. Nobody else does." In a weird way, I had been imposing upon myself an expectation that nobody else cared about. Nobody expected me to wear a coat and tie at Bethany. I was the one who put this on myself because I thought it communicated a professionalism that should go with my position of leadership. I finally started dressing like everyone else at Bethany (business casual is what I call it), and it gave my preaching a new freedom and created a clearer picture for our guests, showing them what our church culture is really like. The most significant issue to me is that our churches provide an atmosphere of grace where we simply do not care if people dress down or dress up. Read the book of James.

116

To turn your average worship service into the complete worship service, develop a game plan for the visual aesthetics in your sanctuary. I believe that big victories are won in small decisions. It is the little things you do that will enhance your worship services. Pay attention to the details.

ten

MUSIC AND THE ARTS

Music and the arts are not the preliminaries but part of the meal we should be savoring. Our minds should be engaged. Our emotions should be stirred. If we are not able to say, "Amen. I think we can go home now," after the music portion, we are shortchanging our people. Our music and art should prompt us to celebrate the Lamb as though we were already in heaven. Another way of thinking about this is that every Sunday should be Resurrection Sunday. It should be another celebration of the life we have in Christ.

MUSIC

One key ingredient in every festive event is music. When I was a professional musician, I played for a lot of weddings. After the ceremony, the reception begins. And with the reception, there is food, friendship, and festivity. This is usually accompanied by music. So it is with the complete worship service. Music adds so much to the atmosphere. It is so powerful that in many Christian movements, music and worship are synonymous. I believe that the music part of the service is worship, but I also believe that the preaching and the other parts of the service are worship too. What we do 24/7 is worship (Rom. 12:1), yet music is a powerful expression of that worship.

MUSIC AND ENERGY

An aspect of music I would like to focus on at this point is the issue of energy. This wonderful creation that God has given us has the potential to alter our emotional world. The people who know this the best are composers of film scores. As I mentioned in *The Complete Worship Leader*, how a composer uses consonance or dissonance can alter mood in foreshadowing, complementing, or resolving a scene in a screenplay. When we are in the movie theater, we know something is about to happen depending on what the composer does melodically, harmonically, or rhythmically.

A significant dynamic of this emotional effect is energy. Music can create or deplete energy. Its power should not be underestimated. All you need to do is perform a little experiment to verify my statement. When you are emotionally low, play some upbeat music, music you really enjoy, and determine if hearing it does not alter your mood. When you are stressed out, play some soothing music to see if you do not experience calm and relaxation. This is the power of music. Right now, as I am writing this, I am listening to a new CD by Ray Charles and Friends that I picked up at Starbucks. This music is very inspirational to me.

Inspiration is exactly what goes on in a worship service. Music lifts our spirits. Music inspires us. Music makes us reflect. Music evokes all kinds of emotions. Therefore, we must ask the questions, How is our song selection providing energy for or extracting energy from our worship service? How are fast and slow songs used in the worship service to create energy? If you put all your fast songs toward the front of the service and all your slow songs prior to the message, will this set up the message with reverse energy? Will it be more difficult to create high-impact messages following an upbeat song or a slow song? Is it better to end the service with a fast song or a slow song? Is it better to start a worship service with a fast song or a slow song? Is it better to do reflective songs or songs of celebration during communion? Of course, the answer to all of these questions is, it depends. It depends on what kind of mood you are trying to create and what kind of energy flow you are producing. You must think through this issue of energy prior to every rehearsal and check and alter the necessary elements in order to get the energy just right.

Music is like insulin. Every diabetic or hypoglycemic knows the impact of insulin. Too much or too little at the wrong time can alter your energy and mood tremendously. It is important to regulate insulin to create sustained energy. Music works the same way. If you give too much of certain elements, you can negatively impact the emotional systems of your worshipers. For example, if you have a whole set of slow music and hymns that sound like dirges, you will crash the system of your worshipers. On the contrary, if you offer nothing but an aerobics class for forty minutes, they will be exhausted from trying to keep up with this kind of energy. The key is to balance out the mood. An awareness of how energy works will help you create the complete worship service.

MUSIC AND MELODY AND RHYTHM

In *The Complete Worship Leader*, I emphasized choosing songs that are easy to learn and hard to forget. I am convinced that the easy-to-learn dynamic of song selection has to do with rhythm. If songs are easy to learn rhythmically, they will be easy to learn. If they are difficult to learn rhythmically, they will be difficult to learn. Never underestimate the importance of "the groove." This is why it is significant to have a first-class percussionist or pianist or guitarist keeping the groove. If a tune is off rhythmically, people will have a tough time learning it.

I have experimented with this over the last twenty-six years. From my days as a professional musician to my days as a worship leader, I have witnessed that singable songs are singable because of what is going on or not going on rhythmically. I am in no way saying that a good, singable song cannot be rhythmically complicated. I am saying that in the melodic line, the rhythm will complement the text syllabically. A good worship tune must follow the rules of good poetry. Words must have a groove. Words must walk, strut, run, and dance. If the words in your worship songs trip over themselves rhythmically, you will not be able to sing the tune.

The reason that many really good worship songs are based on the Psalms is because the Psalms are poetry. The reason that many hymns are so singable is because they are poetic. The reason that many contemporary worship choruses work is simply because they are poetic. Language is a mixing of consonants and vowels in a certain rhythmic pattern. Song is the mixing together of many words forming well-crafted sentences, verses, and choruses. So if you want songs that are easy to learn, ask, "Does this melodic line have rhythm when I speak it or sing it regardless of how it looks on paper?" Ezra Pound said, "Music begins to atrophy when it departs too far from the dance.... Poetry begins to atrophy when it gets too far from music."[1]

The formula for a great song is that it is not only easy to learn but also hard to forget. The hard-to-forget part has to do with melody and meaningful lyrics. Is it memorable? The litmus test is, do you hum or sing that melody throughout the week? This is what makes a great musical. This is what makes a great Disney movie. It is the melody. As a bit of a test, can you hum the melody to the following songs?

- "Over the Rainbow" from *The Wizard of Oz*
- "My Favorite Things" from *The Sound of Music*
- "A Spoonful of Sugar" from *Mary Poppins*
- "Amazing Grace" from your hymnal

How did you do? I am sure you probably could hum or whistle or even sing the melody to those tunes. Now, why is it that you could pull that off? The answer is the melody. The melodic line must enchant our emotional world like a snake charmer moves the cobra. If it does not move us, we will not remember it.

Recently, our worship pastor and I were talking about why so many of the Hillsong Music Australia tunes work so well. Our conclusion was that they are singable. The melodic lines are memorable. This is the key to good songwriting and good song selection. Choose songs people will be singing all week long. Better yet, write them. This is a very important element in the complete worship service.

MUSIC AND THEOLOGY

The text must not only be singable, it must be biblical—biblical not in the sense that it is extracted word for word from the text, but in the sense that it is consistent with what the Bible teaches. In other words, is it theologically responsible? Ask yourself, "What are we teaching our kids as they come to our worship service?" When I come to worship, I want my kids to learn that Christianity is not only relational but also rational. Why do we have to choose between those two options? Why does our worship have to be either theologically correct without expression or with expression but just plain silly? Let us strive for the best of both worlds.

Whether you are a hymn lover or not, one thing you must admit is that most hymns are not theologically illiterate. On

123

the contrary, the hymn writers were trying to shepherd the minds of their congregations because they knew that music is a powerful indoctrination tool. What you sing you remember. And what you remember shapes your worldview.

We are trying to create not only a memorable experience in our worship services but also memorable doctrine for the following week. If we are to communicate the gospel to our generation and to the next generation, then let us strive for theological responsibility in our worship singing.

Back to our hospitality metaphor: How wrong is it to offer a guest a cup of Sanka instead of a cup of Starbucks? How diabolical would it be to offer that coffee with spoiled milk instead of half-and-half? Would you even consider asking your guest if he or she would like some burnt toast with that coffee? Absolutely not! You would offer the very best you could. So it should be with the complete worship service. Give people the best melodies. Give them the best grooves. Give them the best theology. Give them the Word. Give them the gospel. After all, our community is looking for a cup that will never run dry. They are looking for manna that satisfies. They will only be satisfied when they taste and see that the Lord is good. Give them the best.

MUSIC AND THE VOICE OF THE PEOPLE

Every local church is different from every other local church. Certainly we believe the same gospel. Certainly we hold to certain orthodox doctrines that define us as Christians. Certainly we will all spend eternity with each other some day. But until that day, every local church has its own identity, like every person has his or her own fingerprints. This is very significant when it comes to unleashing the arts in the local church.

God has blessed your church with believers who love the Lord with all their hearts, souls, and minds, expressed through

124

their creative abilities. How they lead worship will be different from how the people down the street lead worship. This is good. God created us all unique. Even though we might sing some of the same songs, how we do that will be different. Each church has a unique voice. The trick is to discover that voice. How do you do that?

First of all, pray that God would not only bless your message as you preach or sing this weekend but also give you a love for the people you are preaching to or singing to. Pray that God would open your eyes to see your congregation, not an imaginary congregation or one you see on TV. Pray that God would give you a love for their voices, their laughter, their smiles, their hurt, their pain. This is the starting place for hearing the voice of your congregation.

Second, pray that God would give you prophetic utterances through the preaching of the Word and through the arts that would speak directly to the people he has put in your fellowship. He knows better than anyone else what their needs and concerns are. Pray that God would help you select the choruses your congregation should be singing. God has not called you to download another word from another church to your church. No, there is a special word for your people, at this hour, for your generation. Do not—I repeat—do not regurgitate used material to your people. They need to hear a word from the Lord.

Now, I am not saying that you should never use stories, poetry, film, or music from different sources. As Nancy Beach shares in her wonderful book *An Hour on Sunday*, the arts can be a signpost, a mirror, or a pair of shoes. Art can lead us to God like a signpost. Art can be a mirror revealing the depths of our own souls. And art can be like a pair of shoes in which we walk in someone else's experience for a season, like what we experience every time we watch a movie. Use the best of all the art forms that are available to you, but do it prayerfully.

When you have your creative-arts planning sessions, pray that God would reveal which songs and other ideas you should be using for your people on a given Sunday.

Most of all, enjoy moments of worship with the people you are worshiping with. God loves to hear *your* people sing unto him. He loves to see *your* congregation use their gifts for his glory. He loves to see *your* church use their artistic abilities for his purposes. Remember, the congregation God has asked you to lead has its own voice. Delight yourself in this. Do not wish you were somewhere else in another time and another place. Enjoy what God has for you and your local fellowship.

DRAMA

The most potent effect of adding drama to your worship and arts game plan is that it helps take a sermon (auditory) and make it visual. Drama functions like the ultimate illustration in that people see what you are talking about. The key to adding drama to your ministry is that it has to be excellent, or it will have a negative effect. It is kind of like someone playing the violin: it can bring you to tears if it is good or if it is bad. Therefore, you need to focus on a handful of variables.

First of all, you need someone to either select good dramas or write them. In our case, we have had more success writing our own skits. These are the reasons why: we have a person who is really good at writing, and the skits have been written at a particular time for a particular audience in a particular context. Furthermore, some of our most powerful moments have been when our actors performed the Word. We recently had our drama director perform 1 Corinthians 1 and 3. She did more than recite the text from memory. She created a moment of wonder. She made the Word come alive.

In selecting dramas or skits, you need to start with the big idea of the sermon. This is where your creative-arts team meeting is crucial. At Bethany, we work three to five weeks in advance. When I come up with a series, I share with the creative-arts team the big idea for my sermons and actually read the biblical text. Then we brainstorm. If in the brainstorming time we decide to go with a drama, we have our drama experts either hunt for a drama to fit the message or write their own. Then our drama ministry director recruits the right people to make it happen, and they all get to work.

What I am trying to communicate is that dramas either succeed or fail at the conceptual level. Dramas, for the most part, should set up the sermon. They should create some tension. They should ask a question that the sermon will then answer. If you are using a drama for some reason other than setting up the sermon, then it really needs to fit into the overall theme of the service. Dramas simply do not work in a church context when they are disconnected from the rest of the service, because they fall into the category of entertainment for entertainment's sake.

Dramas also need to be well written. They need to address the issue being raised in the sermon. They need to be emotional: funny, sad, joyful, and so on. They need to overlap with the audience's personal experience or learned experience. This is not unlike giving an illustration in a sermon. The preacher's personal and learned experience needs to overlap with the people's personal and learned experience. If it does not, it is like drinking NyQuil. In a matter of minutes, people will be in la-la land. Drama must captivate the congregation. Drama must enchant them, setting them up for the message.

The next element in making drama work is the actual acting. Just like in your music department, you need to encourage excellence. Our drama director told me that the key to effective dramas is having people with teachable spirits. It is possible to take a person with average acting skills and put him or her in the right part in the right skit, but to do this effectively, you need top-notch leadership. Good leadership is more significant than anything else. It is the drama director who will draw out of the actors what needs to transpire to create the magic for the skit.

Offering workshops and ongoing training for those who are doing skits is also important. Then there is the actual drama in the worship services. People need to memorize parts; that is a given. But they also need to work hard on the delivery. Here is where videotape can work wonders. Videotape all your rehearsals. If something or someone is not working out, make the hard call and make the adjustments before the weekend services. If the drama is not working out in rehearsal, you are only gambling that it will work out on the weekend. You need to see it succeed a handful of times before you actually try to pull it off on the weekend.

The incorporation of drama into your worship services can make a significant contribution to your worship and arts culture when done properly. Pray for God to lead you to the people who desire to use these gifts in creative communication for the glory of God. It is imperative that you have the leadership for effective drama. Do not start this ministry unless you have skilled leadership making average actors great. Once this starts happening on a regular basis, you will notice the difference in the energy of your worship services.

FILM

In a culture where movies are the stories by which we define our lives, it is critical to think through how using film clips can enhance your worship services. This is not difficult for me, because I enjoy film so much. It is very natural for me to make connections between films and the passage from which I am preaching. The little game "This reminds me of . . ." is really easy when it comes to movies. If you are not wired this way, find someone who is.

You must own a license to show film clips. You cannot plead ignorance on this very important legal issue. In the same way you own a CCLI license for music, you must own a license for film. For more information, visit www.CVLI .org or www.screenvue.com.

The reason film clips work so well in creating the complete worship service is that they bring abstract concepts down to the concrete level. In film, all of the arts are combined. You have screenwriting, acting, musical composition, costuming, sets. The list goes on and on.

I have heard some people say that preaching just cannot compete with the movie industry, and therefore, you need to be cautious about using movie clips. The bottom line is that the Word of God is not in competition with anything, especially Hollywood. Film clips are used as a servant to the text, not as a competitive tool. The Word of God not only informs but also performs and transforms.[2] Have confidence in the Word of God. Props, movie clips, drama, or any other medium is there simply to support the message. The arts should be used to enhance the Word of God in the worship service. I am saying all of this because I attended a conference once where a screenwriter emphasized that preaching just could not compete with Hollywood. The screenwriter was well intentioned; he was trying to teach us the importance of story, but this brother was really confused about the power of the spoken Word. People come to faith by *hearing* the Word of God.

Here are a few cautions about using film clips. First of all, make sure the clip is not too long, or it will break the flow of the sermon. Second, it must fit the point exactly, or it will seem like the pastor is lazy and relying on a movie to make up for poor preparation. If you cannot move people with words, do not use film clips to help this deficiency. Lastly, the clip must be appropriate. Do not use film clips just for a joke to get a laugh. I did this once with a *Saturday Night Live* clip, and it backfired on me.

PAINTING

Painting has the opposite effect of film and drama. It pauses chronological time and promotes transcendence. Whereas drama and film tend to bring the abstract to the concrete, good painting does just the opposite. Painting can create more mystery in your worship services. This is good.

I recently had breakfast with Peter Hiett, author of *Eternity Now: Encountering the Jesus of Revelation*. Peter is a pastor at Lookout Mountain Community Church, just outside of Denver. He is a gifted narrative preacher with a tremendous infusion of the poetic weaved into his system. As an attendee of Lookout Mountain Community Church, Philip Yancey said that, week in and week out, Peter Hiett is one the best teachers he has ever heard.

I asked Peter about his preaching orientation, from how he prepares to how he delivers, and he shared with me a very important insight. He said, "Kevin, the problem with so much of evangelical preaching is that we try to explain the mystery all the time. I think maybe we are called to simply guard the mystery." Now, what I heard Peter saying is that we work so hard at making everything understandable in the worship service that we lose the transcendence of our worship service much of the time.

Paintings have a way of creating transcendence. When you go to an art gallery, the interpretation is not laid out for you. There might be a brief explanation of the artist and the name of the painting, but the interpretation is left to the one beholding the portrait. The same thing can take place in your sanctuary. Incorporating painting into your worship time can add so much.

This last year I preached a short series on Jonah. I took one chapter a week and finished the book in a month. But it was a significant series for me in this regard: we incorporated painting into my messages. A gifted painter in our congregation, Jami Adams, painted a mural of a ship in the middle of a storm the first week. You could feel that storm by looking at the painting. As I talked about Jonah's disobedience, there was this giant painting capturing the congregation in a moment of time. The next week, there was a mural of a giant fish next to the painting of the ship. The third week, a mural of a mass of people repenting at the message of Jonah showed up on the platform. And then the fourth week, a mural of Jonah sitting under a withering plant, sulking, appeared. Wow! This was a fantastic experience! Jami captured in these murals the big idea of the message, yet there was a tremendous amount of room for the congregation to use their own imaginations.

Whether painting is used to enhance a message or to create a sense of wonder in your sanctuary, making the decision to engage in this art form will pay off in a very significant way. You will, of course, have to have some kind of screening process. You want to keep your standard of quality and excellence high.

BULLETINS

I learned from our pastor of worship and arts that finding someone to design your own bulletins and creating a new look for each new series is another way for artistic expression to be experienced in the local church. Why should bulletins be boring? Why not add a little creative art into this aspect of the service as well? Find someone who has experience, and let them use their gifts for the glory of God.

131

POETRY AND LITERATURE

I remember Eugene Peterson saying that the reason he read poetry was because poets are the custodians of words, and those who preach the Word need to care about words. I believe the kind of poetry used in your worship services will either enhance or detract. I personally think poetry is like humor. Either it fits or it is off. All I can say is that it is always a risk to quote a poem in your worship service, for the simple reason that people may not get it.

I have even tried to quote from some of my favorite modern poets like Billy Collins, but it has not worked very well in my context. I remember quoting a poem called "The Art of Drowning" by Billy Collins, and people gave me the deer-in-the-headlights look. It was a *Blues Brothers* moment when everyone sits in silence looking at you like you landed from another planet.

When I mention my own struggles about poetry, please do not hear me saying not to ever read poems out loud. All I am saying is that you always run the risk of poetry disconnecting with a culture that does not understand poetry. I believe the exception is the postmodern generation. They appreciate poetry and really enjoy poems in the worship service.

Concerning reading literature, I learned from one of my preaching professors, Earl Palmer, that if you are going to quote or read a section out of a literary work, then read it straight from the book. This enhances credibility that an author, like a G. K. Chesterton, in fact wrote those words. It is imperative to expose our congregations to these great thinkers whenever their ideas are relevant. Too many people are turned off by the church because they think we are armed with glib expressions and thoughtless rhetoric.

Furthermore, we are increasingly becoming an illiterate society. When all is said and done, there is little difference between the person who cannot read and the person who does not. In the church, we need to reclaim loving God will all of our mind.

Many great writers have interacted with the important themes we are dealing with in our sermons. If we can assimilate their thoughts into our worship services, this might encourage someone to read the book we quoted. The consequence might turn out to be someone learning to love the Lord with all his or her mind.

DANCE

An art form that is being explored more and more in the worship service is dance. I first experienced dance in worship at the Anaheim Vineyard back in 1987. Of course, there are many different approaches to dance. There is celebratory dance, like you would experience in a Messianic congregation. This is where groups of dancers come up toward the front of the sanctuary and lead in dance to remind the congregation that the Lord our God is a mighty deliverer. Typically, these dances are done in circles to very upbeat music. The Israelites' dance is an example of celebrative dance. "Then Miriam the prophetess, Aaron's sister, took a tambourine in her hand, and all the women followed her, with tambourines and dancing. Miriam sang to them: 'Sing to the LORD, for he is highly exalted. The horse and its rider he has hurled into the sea'" (Exod. 15:20–21).

A different approach is interpretive dance. Interpretive dances are choreographed to match the lyrics of a song. Similar to drama, all dance forms make people weep because they are either excellent or embarrassing. A lot of work needs to go into making dance special.

In general, I have found that dance works best when attention is not drawn to it. Now, occasionally you might do a special number where there is no audience participation and the dance helps communicate the message of the special number. But if dance is used in worship, it is best done when people are singing. Our goal is to create a culture of worship in the complete worship service. This means that dance might be in the aisles; it might be up front, not on the platform. Or if you have a big enough platform when factoring in all the musicians, you might have the dancers on the platform. But their dance would happen during a praise song while everyone else is engaged. Believe me, this can be very powerful. In addition, incorporate children into the dance team. Again, the Bible encourages dance. "Let Israel rejoice in their Maker; let the people of Zion be glad in their King. Let them praise his name with dancing and make music to him with tambourine and harp. For the LORD takes delight in his people; he crowns the humble with salvation" (Ps. 149:2–4).

OPENNESS TO CREATIVE EXPRESSION

Above all, I encourage you to be open to creative expression. Only dead fish swim with the stream. Tanya Wheway said,

Inspiration cannot be forced. Sometimes it simply comes like a bolt out of the blue; at other times it totally refuses to come out to play. There are times, however, when we can cajole it into action by freeing our minds—listening to some beautiful music, spending time in a beautiful garden, meditating, reading, exposing ourselves to a new environment or spending time with positive, passionate and creative people.[3]

The best thing that happened to our church this last year was the formulation of a creative-arts team. The team attended the Willow Creek Arts Conference, and things started to happen big time when they returned. Hands down, that

134

conference did more for our worship services this year than any other conference. The team was motivated and inspired to try new ways of approaching the worship service and to incorporate some practical tools on a weekly basis.

Currently, the team consists of me, our pastor of worship and arts, a vocal director, a visual-arts director, a drama director, and a couple who provide tremendous insight into creative expression, technical issues, and scriptwriting. As soon as we discuss the big idea of the text, we start thinking of songs, films, dramas, visual pictures, and moods we would like to create and a host of other creative ideas we could never find in a book. This is our outlet for creative expression. We must empower artists in our own churches to offer the congregation a taste of heaven.

> Christians so gifted by God should be composing music and telling stories about life—emotions, events, experiences, and so forth—that exhibit the kind of understanding and insight into these affairs that comes from a faith vision. Artists and critics alike should look to find the ways in which the cosmic struggle between good and evil takes place in everyday life and help others to see that. Artworks that are characteristically Christian should be clues to what life is like in God's world.[4]

How do your artists find opportunities to use their creative communication gifts for the glory of God? You must answer this question if you want to develop the complete worship service. Not embracing the arts in your worship service results in an incomplete worship service. Over and over again we are told in the Scriptures to worship the Lord in spirit, in truth, with everything that is within us, with all kinds of instruments, with dance, and by singing a new song unto the Lord. The bottom line is that all the arts exist to glorify God. Therefore, engage everything the Lord has put at your disposal for his glory. Let the people of God praise the name of the Lord.

eleven

THE WORD OF GOD

In this chapter, I will address the importance of our people receiving a well-prepared meal by feasting on the Word. The Word is the main course. The church is famished for good Bible teaching. Anything that substitutes for the Bible as the food we digest in the worship service is processed food. We need the Word of God. Furthermore, we need preaching that gives Good News and not just good advice. There is a sickness permeating Christianity today, and this sickness is the lack of understanding that the pulpit exists to give the hope of the solid rock of Christ and not advice under the law. If our preaching would not get us kicked out of a synagogue or mosque, it is probably not Christian. Give people the written Word of God and the living Word of God.

WHERE'S THE BEEF?

I recently was interviewed by an individual who has been coming to our church with his wife. He wanted to meet with me because he had some theological questions he wanted to ask me—thirty-eight questions to be specific. He wanted to know if I believed in the virgin birth. He wanted to know if I believed that Jesus is the only way to the Father. He wanted to know if I believed in the infallibility of the Word of God. The questions went on and on. I felt as if I were in an ordination council. But it was not a professor asking me these questions. It was not a district superintendent. No, it was a person with no seminary background dying to find a pastor who believed in the Bible. He came from a movement that was more interested in discussing the ordination of homosexuals than how to be a devoted follower of Jesus Christ. He showed me a recent small group study he had been going through that focused entirely on the gay agenda. When I heard this man's story, my heart just broke. He told me that he had heard more Bible and gospel preaching in forty-five minutes at our church than he had heard in the last decade in his previous church. After hearing this brother's story, I want to make a plea to my fellow pastors to preach the Word!

THE WORD OF GOD IS THE MAIN COURSE

In the complete worship service, the Word of God is the main course. If we are giving people a taste of the wedding banquet at the end of the age, then we need to help them realize that people do not live on bread alone but by every word that proceeds from the mouth of God. It is the Word that nourishes our souls. We might have had a nice appetizer and salad with the arts, but the Word of God has to be the meat and potatoes in a worship service. If not, maybe we have worshiped or maybe we have not, but without the Word, the worship service is incomplete. We come to worship not only to tell the Lord how much we appreciate him but also to hear his voice. Remember what the Bible teaches about making the Word of God a priority in public worship.

Command and teach these things. Don't let anyone look down on you because you are young, but set an example for the believers in speech, in life, in love, in faith and in purity. Until I come, *devote yourself to the public reading of Scripture, to preaching and to teaching.* Do not neglect your gift, which was given you through a prophetic message when the body of elders laid their hands on you.

Be diligent in these matters; give yourself wholly to them, so that everyone may see your progress. *Watch your life and doctrine closely.* Persevere in them, because if you do, you will save both yourself and your hearers.

1 Timothy 4:11–16, italics added

Am I saying that music and the arts are only warm-ups for the preaching of the Word of God? Absolutely not! Am I saying that a service without an emphasis on the preaching of the Word of God is dysfunctional? Absolutely! Our primary objective in a worship service is to come into the presence of God, hear his voice, and respond to him in praise and then in obedience. Our primary objective is not just to awaken the aesthetic in the human soul as though we were the next alternative to the art gallery, the movie theater, or the concert hall. Our primary objective is to meet God. And how offended would you be if someone invited you out for lunch and they talked the entire time and never once heard your voice? I think you would say you had been used. Quite frankly, I wonder if God does not feel used in our worship services. We sing and engage our hearts, minds, and souls to talk about God, but then when it comes to hearing God speak, there are those who tell us anything over a twenty- to thirty-minute sermon is too much. People do not want to listen to someone speak; they want to watch movies and be entertained. Have we asked God about our apathy toward his voice?

It seems to me that if the apostle Paul encouraged Timothy to devote himself to reading Scripture, teaching, and preaching, we should pay attention to this advice as well. Jesus was a teacher. The apostles were teachers. They gave themselves to prayer and the ministry of the Word. If we want to see our worship services go to the next level, we need to passionately care about the ministry of the Word.

VERSE BY VERSE OR VERSE WITH VERSE?

When we finally agree on the importance of the preaching of the Word of God, the question that usually follows is, do I preach verse *by* verse or verse *with* verse? (Verse-by-verse preaching is usually referred to as Bible preaching. Verse-with-verse preaching is usually referred to as topical preaching.)[1] Some would make the argument that preaching verse with verse is absolutely imperative if you are trying to reach the unchurched. Therefore, the verse with verse is for weekend preaching. Then the verse by verse is for believers and, therefore, for weekday preaching. Personally, I do not think it matters if you are a verse-by-verse or a verse-with-verse person.

I do think, however, it matters that you are expositional and not impositional. Expositional preaching exposes what is in the text. Impositional preaching imposes upon the text what is not there. There are some preachers who pride themselves on being verse-by-verse people, but they are unfaithful to the text, because in their analysis paralysis, they miss the context of the passage and, therefore, impose an illegitimate interpretation upon the text. The same could be said for the verse-with-verse preacher. You can cut and paste verses together to support your argument, but the question remains: could your argument be better made with a passage of Scripture that actually makes the argument you are making? The answer is yes. Therefore, the most important task is to be faithful to the Word, whether you are dealing with one verse, one narrative, or one chapter.

THE WRITTEN WORD OF GOD

The written Word of God in our worship services is absolutely a must in this day and age of pluralism. Our people are getting confused in a culture with so much ideology of what is right and wrong, true and false, or good and bad. Is it no wonder the psalmist said that the person who meditates on the law day and night would be like a tree firmly planted by streams of water, which yields its fruit in its season and whose leaf does not wither. In whatever such a person does, he or she prospers (Ps. 1:2–3). The reality is that there is a biblical illiteracy going unchallenged in our evangelical churches today.

We need to raise the value of studying the Bible to the body of Christ. In our Bible studies, we need to actually study the Bible and not every new curriculum that substitutes for the Bible in the name of being a Bible study. We need to take time to open our Bibles in our worship services. We need to use our Bibles when we preach. If the congregation does not see the pastors open their Bibles when they preach, how will they ever get the message that studying the Bible is a priority?

We need to teach the written Word of God in the complete worship service. "In the pulpit we are expositors, not authors."[2] There is simply no substitute for expositional preaching. I do not care how well you can weave a story together and make people laugh or move people to tears. If you do not give them the Scriptures, they will not grow in the faith. "Consequently, faith comes from hearing the message, and the message is heard through the word of Christ" (Rom. 10:17). David Buttrick has said it perfectly in his book *Homiletic: Moves and Structures*:

> The malaise is odd in view of our heritage. Whatever our Christian stance, we are children of Saint Paul, of Chrysostom, of Augustine, perhaps of Luther. So when Saint Paul states flat out that "faith comes from hearing" (Rom. 10:17), should we

141

correct him by suggesting that faith comes from visual aids, and visual aids from your nearest religious publishing house? Or when Martin Luther declares, "The Word, I say, and the Word alone is bearer of God's grace," shall we refer him to a book on body language? Nothing is more peculiar than the church's loss of confidence in language. Do not Christians insist that God "spoke" and the world was; that God tossed the Word like a burning coal to scald the lips of prophets; that the Word became flesh and spoke good news; that the church is built on testimony of apostles, martyrs, and saints? Yet, today, we stammer. About the only people left who do believe in the power of words are poets and revolutionaries. We, a people of the Word, are wordless.[3]

We need to regain momentum by teaching the Bible. We need to regain our confidence in the written Word of God. The written Word of God not only informs, it performs and transforms. When Jesus told Lazarus to come forth, we must ask the question, how do dead people hear? Well, the answer is that dead people cannot hear. But the Word of God is so powerful that it can cause a dead person to hear.[4] Every weekend, dead people are at your church. Do you really want to see life breathed into them? Then teach the Word of God.

THE LIVING WORD OF GOD

As much as we should care about teaching the Scriptures, we should also care about preaching Christ. You see, we must not only *teach* the written Word but also *preach* the living Word. What makes Christian preaching different from social and political commentary or psychological babble is that it is about a person. And that person is not me. It is not you. It is Christ. Christian preaching must center on Christ being the solution. Certainly, we must spell out the problems. But the solution is not to pull ourselves up by our bootstraps and get our acts together. That is not the gospel. The gospel is that Christ in us is the answer. It is not just about the imitation of Christ but about the habitation of Christ.

I am convinced that people are literally dying for Good News. The people I am talking about are not only the sinners in your community but also the saints in your fellowship. They already know what they are not doing. They already know that their report card is not anything to brag about. How disheartening to come to church and be reminded that you are flunking and you need to try harder. This is so demoralizing. It is kind of like telling people who just lost their jobs that they should have tried harder. I am not exaggerating when I say that a lot of preaching uses this kind of moralism.

Good News is so different. First of all, Good News is not about us being the solution but about Christ being the solution. It is not about us being better; it is about the fruit of the Spirit. It is not about us trying to please God but about us trusting God to live his life through us.

When sinners in your community hear this message, they will start flooding to your church. Trust me; I was saved at Calvary Chapel during a time when people were flooding to hear the gospel message. I have seen it happen all over the world. When you fly the flag and tell people that being born again is a work of the Spirit of God and that he is the one who wants to give life and life abundantly, you will not be able to keep sinners from coming to the church. What an unbeliever is really opposed to is the moralism so prevalent in our churches. They know they are a mess. They just do not want to come to a place where they are reminded week after week *without any solution*. Give people the solution. It does not take a leader to preach the problem. It does take one to offer a solution. Jesus Christ is the solution.

The believers who come to your church have been beat up all week long. They need to hear a message of hope. They need to be reminded that Jesus is lovesick over them. They need to be reminded that Jesus will never leave them or forsake them. They need to be reminded that he who began a good work in them will continue to complete it until the day of Christ Jesus. They need to be reminded that they are resident aliens and that this is not their home. They need to be reminded that they are citizens of the kingdom of God, not of this world. They need to be reminded that they are about to receive an inheritance that will never fade away. Tell them who they are in Christ. Remind the saints that they are saints. This is the job of preaching. If you offer *didache* (teaching ethics), root it in the *kerygma* (preaching Christ). "The Church needs men who, knowing the world around them, and knowing the Christ above them and within, will set the trumpet of the Gospel to their lips, and proclaim His sovereignty and all-sufficiency."[5]

APPLICATION OR IMPLICATION?

This, then, begs the questions, how much should we emphasize application of the text? What if there is no application but rather an implication? Evangelical preaching is so obsessed with the need to apply everything that we are shifting into just another moral religion. Yes, you heard me right. Every religion has a game plan. Pick any religion. They all have a game plan for following God. The problem with every religion is that they have not factored in the high priest variable. You see, without a high priest, it is impossible to get represented before a holy God. This is where Christianity comes in. Jesus is that High Priest. That is why every text has to eventually lead to Jesus, or Christianity becomes just another religion offering good advice. Bryan Chapell, in his wonderful book *Christ-Centered Preaching*, states:

A message that merely advocates morality and compassion remains sub-Christian even if the preacher can prove that the Bible demands such behaviors. By ignoring the sinfulness of man that makes even our best works tainted before God and by neglecting the grace of God that makes obedience possible and acceptable, such messages necessarily subvert the Christian message. Christian preachers often do not recognize this impact of their words because they are simply recounting a behavior clearly specified in the text in front of them. But a message that even inadvertently teaches others that their works win God's acceptance inevitably leads people away from the Gospel. Moral maxims and advocacy of ethical conduct fall short of the requirements of biblical preaching.[6]

In our obsession with application, we must realize that the only thing we might come away with in a worship service is an implication. Maybe the implication is simply that God loves us and will never leave us or forsake us. There might not be any application related to this fact for the week.

Now, you might ask, "Why are you going on about this issue?" For this simple reason: a worship service is to celebrate the work of Christ. It is to declare the mighty acts of God. It is not to celebrate what we have done. It is to celebrate not our dedication to God but rather his dedication to us. So what I am trying to say is that the closer preaching is to worship, the more theologically sound it will be. The more we emphasize the work of Christ, the more worshipful our preaching will be. The more we take every text to the Christ events, the more accurate our evangelical pulpits will be. James Stewart criticized this epidemic of good-advice preaching when he said:

> The Kingdom of Heaven was not, as Jesus and the apostles had proclaimed it, a gift of God breaking into history from the beyond: it was a human achievement, the product of social amelioration, culture and scientific planning. Jesus Himself,

according to this view, was the Pioneer of progress, the supreme Leader, the apex of the vanguard of the pilgrim host
of humanity—not a terrific Being shattering history with the
explosive word, "Before Abraham was, I am." Christianity
sounded in men's ears as good advice, rather than good news:
an exhortation to be up and doing, to fight the good fight
and follow the gleam, not the announcement of something
which God had already done, decisively and for ever. There
was accordingly an inclination to regard the preacher as the
purveyor of religious homilies and ethical uplift, not the herald
of the mighty acts of God.[7]

OFFERING HOPE IN CHRIST

Correlated with preaching Christ is the need to offer hope.
If I know all the things I have not done, and then I come to
church and hear more things I have not done, there is no
hope in this message. On the other hand, if I come to church
and hear about what Christ is doing, I am infused with hope.
When I am reminded of who I am in Christ, my hope is
renewed. When I hear that he who began a good work in
me will continue to complete it until the day of Christ Jesus,
I am filled with hope. When I hear that Christ is not done
with me, but rather the Spirit of God is making me more like
the Son every day and every season of my life, I am renewed
with hope.

People are coming to our churches, and they desperately
need hope. Hope comes from hearing the gospel correctly
proclaimed. Good News gives hope. Good advice produces
despair. When we promote hope, we will connect with the
essence of the complete worship service. The essence of the
complete worship service is a celebration of what Christ has
done for us and the realization that he has invited us to be at
his table. It is a celebration that his banner over us is love.

Never dumb down the teaching of the Scriptures or the preaching of Christ. The Word of God is living and active. And the living Word is calling the weary from your community to come unto him and find rest. The complete worship service is more than a quality service. The complete worship service is the banquet table where we hear once again of Christ's love for us. In the next chapter, we will focus on the Eucharist, the perfect response to the ministry of the Word.

twelve

THE EUCHARIST

In many churches today, if you miss the Good Friday service, you have missed the communion service. If we preach the gospel, it makes sense to celebrate the gospel through a time at the table. The greatest loss in our neglect of the table is not only failure to celebrate what Christ has done for us but also lack of preparation for the wedding feast. Eucharist needs to be explained for a new generation and celebrated in anticipation of our going home to be with our Lord. If we are celebrating a nice meal, the Eucharist would definitely be the dessert. This cannot be omitted from the complete worship service.

WHAT DOES *EUCHARIST* MEAN?

Eucharist means "giving thanks." When we take time to celebrate the Lord's Table, we are giving thanks to God for sending his Son Jesus Christ to die for us. When we come around the table, we are giving thanks that our sins have been paid not in part but in full. When we gather around the table, we are giving thanks that we have been redeemed by the blood of the Lamb. When we come around the table, we are giving thanks that the wrath of God has been appeased. When we come around the table, we are giving thanks that we will spend eternity in his presence. Eucharist is the giving of thanks.

A word like *Eucharist* can sound too liturgical for evangelical ears. Therefore, we talk about the ordinance of the Lord's Supper. Evangelicals are uncomfortable with the Catholic connotation of the sacrament of the Eucharist, which is the climax of the mass. But in all of our fuss, we have slipped into neglect. And in our neglect, we are missing something vital to worship. When we worship, we are celebrating the work of Christ. And what better way to do this than to break bread and drink from the cup that reminds us of the body and blood of our Lord?

THE PERFECT RESPONSE

The Eucharist is the perfect response to the Word if the Word is preached as gospel. If in our preaching we are magnifying the work of Christ, coming around the table is our way of saying thanks. In Christ-centered preaching, we are reminded of the grace and mercy of God. As our hearts and minds are stirred with the thought that we have been bought with a price, we long for a way to say thank you. The best way to do that is to celebrate the Eucharist.

CELEBRATING THE WORK OF CHRIST

The neglect of the Eucharist needs to be remedied because the gospel is being hijacked by good advice. Quite honestly, I see no reason to come to the table if our message is, fix your life by pulling yourself up by the bootstraps. I see no reason to give thanks to Jesus Christ for his work if the real message of the morning is that my dedication to him could be improved. I see no reason to break bread and drink the cup if all I need to do to be a better Christian is to be more disciplined.

On the other hand, if every text leads us to Christ, then celebrating the work of Christ is appropriate and essential. If I realize that the Hebrew Bible points to Jesus Christ and that my Lord is the fulfillment of the prophesied kingdom, then celebrating the work of Christ is imperative.

Since Jesus said to his disciples that they were to do this in remembrance of him, then we should make sure that our worship services celebrate the work of Christ as well. I simply cannot overemphasize this point: the complete worship service is a service dedicated to celebrating Jesus Christ and the kingdom of God.

HEALING LIFE'S HURTS AT THE TABLE

In our introductory class to our church, we spend some time reflecting on our association with the Evangelical Free Church of America. Consequently, we spend time going through our twelve-point doctrinal statement. When we get to article 7, which deals with baptism and the Lord's Supper, we spend some time discussing the theological positions of how various movements think about the Lord's Supper. There are basically three positions: transubstantiation, consubstantiation, and memorial. Like many evangelical churches, we tend to take the memorial position in that we do not think anything supernatural happens to the actual elements.

On the other hand, I do believe that something supernatural happens in every worship service, especially worship services where the Eucharist is observed. In my own experience as a pastor, I have seen more tears shed during time around the table than in other times of the worship service. Believers come to worship lacking hope, and then they come to the table where life's hurts (in this case, despair) are healed at that moment.

Abuse, neglect, despair, depression, divorce, and every other kind of sin in the heart of humanity are addressed when the gospel is preached and celebrated. For example, believers who are going through divorce because their spouses abandoned them for other people have heard me say, "If you are born again by the Spirit of God, Christ will never leave you or forsake you." The moment those words are heard and celebrated, something significant takes place. Namely, they give thanks that Christ will never abandon them like their spouses did. You tell me, do you believe life's hurts are healed when this kind of experience happens in a worship service? Never, ever underestimate the power of meaningful celebrations of breaking bread and drinking from the cup as it pertains to pastoral theology. People are nurtured and shepherded through these kinds of experiences.

ANTICIPATING THE WEDDING BANQUET

During our age, which is really the end times, we are proclaiming the kingdom of God. We are telling people all over the world that the rule of God is an easy yoke and that although there will be persecution in this world, there is no better way to experience the blessing of God than to be in the kingdom of God. As a part of this proclamation, we declare with everything that is within us that there will be a wedding banquet. And in these last days, the ultimate act of hospitality has been displayed: Christ is inviting all those who are undeserving to partake at his table. Christ wants to bless the very people who have cursed him. He wants to invite everyone to the banquet. Unfortunately, the paradox of the kingdom of God is that the very people who you would think would embrace such an invitation have rejected it. Therefore, the invitation is extended to those who really know what a blessing this would be. They in turn have accepted and are continuing to accept this invitation. The wedding banquet at the end of the age is about to start. And until the time of that perfected kingdom, we look forward with anticipation.

Every time we come to the table to celebrate, we not only look backward in time but look forward as well. You see, every Eucharist is not only a memorial but also an anticipation:

> For I received from the Lord what I also passed on to you: The Lord Jesus, on the night he was betrayed, took bread, and when he had given thanks, he broke it and said, "This is my body, which is for you; do this in remembrance of me." In the same way, after supper he took the cup, saying, "This cup is the new covenant in my blood; do this, whenever you drink it, in remembrance of me." For whenever you eat this bread and drink this cup, you proclaim the Lord's death *until he comes*."
>
> 1 Corinthians 11:23–26, italics added

This is the part that needs to be added to all of our introductory classes in our churches. We need to remind people that we are not only remembering the Lord and what he did at Calvary but also anticipating the Lord and what the perfected kingdom will look like. If you take what I have just said to heart, your average worship service will become the complete worship service in atmosphere, experience, and impact on your people. Remember, saints and sinners are both looking for the same thing when they come to church this weekend: hope!

FINISHING OFF THE MEAL WELL

When you go to a fine restaurant, the kind where you are really dishing out the cash, you want to taste a very important aspect of that meal: the dessert. Yes, you want to have the coffee and the dessert. Then you will know that your wonderful meal has come to a conclusion.

My wife and I have a favorite restaurant here in the Denver area that we go to on our anniversary. The name of the restaurant is The Broker. You pay one price for your meal, but your meal includes a bowl of shrimp with cocktail sauce, bread, salad, main course, coffee, and dessert. All the elements of the meal are important for this special anniversary tradition we have.

I believe that celebrating the Lord's Supper is like having dessert at the end of a fine meal. Now, I know there will be some who will object to my analogy. In some traditions, there will be those who will argue, "No, it's not the dessert; it's the main course." But bear with me in this analogy for a moment. First of all, in many evangelical churches, Eucharist is simply neglected. The same is true in many charismatic renewal churches. I know from firsthand experience. I spent a decade in the charismatic renewal movement. I have spent the last fourteen years in the evangelical movement. Yet, as I have already mentioned, I grew up Catholic.

For traditions where the Eucharist is a priority, praise the Lord. You keep going. Keep the Lord's Supper as the main course. But for charismatic and evangelical churches, I want you to begin to think of your worship services as a nice dinner at The Broker. I want you to think of every aspect of the meal as significant. In the same way you have an appetizer, bread, and salad, I want you to think about music and arts as this delicious part of the meal. In the same way you have a main course, I want you to think about the preaching of the Word of God as the main course. For both charismatics and evangelicals, this is not difficult. Yet I would like to encourage you to add that final touch to your meal. Do not forget about the dessert. I want you to think of the Eucharist as dessert. Can you do without dessert? I guess. Is a fine meal better with dessert? Absolutely! Can you have dessert once a month? Better than once a year! But wouldn't it be fantastic if you could have dessert every week? Absolutely!

I want to encourage you to celebrate a full-course meal. Do not leave out any element. Celebration of every part is the key to the complete worship service. Sure, you can pull off any old kind of service. But why not go the extra mile? Why not put your best foot forward every weekend? Why not do it all for the glory of God? As you begin to think about this glorious opportunity, do not waste one Sunday. Give it your very best for Christ and for his bride.

FEASTING ON CHRIST

When we come to worship, may we feast on Christ. May we sing about Christ. May we express the mercy of Christ in our art. May we preach about Christ. And may we gather around the table to remember what he did for us at Calvary and to anticipate his coming. Every worship service must be a feast. The complete worship service will settle for nothing less.

PART FOUR

TALKING ABOUT A TASTE OF HEAVEN

thirteen

THANKSGIVING AS THE CONSUMMATION OF JOY

It was C. S. Lewis who taught us that thanksgiving is the consummation of joy. When people go to a movie and really like it, they just have to go and tell someone. When people go to a fine restaurant and have a wonderful experience, it will not be long until someone else is having that experience. Why? It is because someone recommended that restaurant to all their friends. The key to the complete worship service is for people to gossip the gospel as the result of coming to church. People should be telling others about their foretaste of heaven. And if it is true that people are ultimately looking for that place where there will be no more dying, and if it is true that your church tells people of this place and allows them to experience firsthand what this place looks like, it most likely will not be long before a spirit of invitation will permeate your people.

THOUGHTS FROM C. S. LEWIS

C. S. Lewis made a wonderful observation about praise.

I think we delight to praise what we enjoy because the praise not merely expresses but completes the enjoyment; it is its appointed consummation. It is not out of compliment that lovers keep on telling one another how beautiful they are; the delight is incomplete till it is expressed. It is frustrating to have discovered a new author and not to be able to tell anyone how good he is; to come suddenly, at the turn of the road, upon some mountain valley of unexpected grandeur and then to have to keep silent because the people with you care for it no more than for a tin can in the ditch; to hear a good joke and find no one to share it with (the perfect hearer died a year ago).[1]

The application to the complete worship service is obvious. If what you do in your worship services brings great delight to those who come to your church, they will talk to others about the experience. Remember when I said that churches grow like restaurants grow? Because it is natural for human beings to complete their joy through spontaneous praise, the best marketing you can do for your church is to do all things well. Give the body of Christ a fantastic experience of worshiping the Lord, and they will be back. Furthermore, they will be back with others. This is the way church growth works on a practical level.

The next point worth noting is that healthy people tend to praise most. So the question of the hour is, does your church represent cranky people or healthy people? This is a very important question simply because it impacts your church health. Either your church has a magnetic pull because the people are grateful and therefore filled with praise, or it has a distancing effect because the people are sick and complaining.

160

Those with the most capacious minds are the ones who praise most. They always find something to praise. They are full of life and express their joy by praising. On the other hand, the cranks and misfits are always complaining about everything.[2]

Now, it must be noted that complaining is not the same thing as having a critical mind. It is quite possible to have a critical mind without having a critical spirit. That is what we should strive for as pastors, and that is what we should pray for in the local church. People who have critical minds without critical spirits promote church health.

The complete worship service is ultimately filled with people who love the Lord and are excited about sharing that love with others. The complete worship service is permeated by a positive, deeply appreciative spirit that ultimately spills over into the community. The complete worship service is a place where memories are made on a regular basis. There is always a wow factor. This is how healthy, growing, multiplying churches operate. Praise is simply in the DNA.

PEOPLE WILL REMEMBER HOW YOU MADE THEM FEEL

Four years ago, I went through a very traumatic experience. One day while sitting down at the piano and singing some praise choruses, I noticed my voice was not functioning. This had been happening off and on for about a month, but on this particular day, my voice would not work at all.

I went to get it checked out. Initially, I thought it was a bug or, worst-case scenario, a bit of laryngitis. What I discovered turned out to be far worse. I ended up meeting with a laryngologist and discovered that I had nodules on my vocal chords. Many reasons were cited: overuse of my voice, dehydration, and even acid reflux. Supposedly, just a bit of acidity was causing my larynx to enlarge, which created a home for nodules.

I was placed on a strict diet and was told not to talk. Whispering was even worse than talking. I had to refrain from singing or speaking for the next three months. I was devastated, because I had a week of teaching I was planning to do in the Czech Republic, not to mention all of the worship leading I was doing. I quickly enlisted worship leaders and teachers to cover my responsibilities.

In addition to all of that, I had to go through vocal therapy. These sessions were not singing lessons or vocal training to improve intonation, articulation, and inflection. These were intense sessions of vocal therapy. In the midst of my rehab, my therapist said something that has stuck with me ever since. We were discussing my vocation and the ministry of the gospel when she said, "You know, Kevin, people will not remember everything you told them, but they will remember how you made them feel." This statement was both an epiphany and demoralizing at the same time. As someone who cares very much about content and the fact that the Word of God is alive, I felt somewhat threatened by this comment. But I still could not shake the reality of what she said.

That day I resolved to continue to work really hard on content but to always remember that people will remember how I made them feel. I realized that communication for me was as much about how I said something as it was about what I said. This meant that I needed to allow people to experience the sermon with all of their senses, not just their hearing. I started preaching sermons in character. If I was talking about the Light coming into the darkness, I preached a sermon in complete darkness. One Sunday, to illustrate the liberation Jesus came to give us, I was led into the sanctuary, handcuffed and dressed in an orange jumpsuit, by a police officer. The climax happened at the end of the sermon when the police officer removed the handcuffs and tossed them into the middle aisle. At that moment, I declared that we are set free from bondage and that Christ came to give us freedom. The examples could go on and on, but the point is that people remembered how I made them feel.

Correlated with this, we hired a worship pastor whose creative abilities never cease to amaze me. Every week the sanctuary looks different. Every week we seek to give people a new experience. Now, we have had a few critics. But the fact remains that we have added lots of people to our worship attendance since we started doing this. People are coming to Christ. People are being baptized. The dechurched are being reengaged in the life of faith. Of course, there are many variables to this phenomenon, but I believe a key ingredient has been the desire we have as a creative-arts team to give our people a new experience every Sunday.

If you give people a fresh experience every time they come to worship, they will talk about these experiences. If you do it with the intent of helping people understand the Good News of Jesus Christ and the kingdom of God and not of just providing entertainment, the Holy Spirit will put his hand of blessing on your worship service. I believe with everything that is within me that the complete worship service is not just a cognitive experience but a multisensory experience. Help people hear, see, touch, smell, and taste the kingdom of heaven. This is done through the arts, through the experiential preaching of the Word, and through Eucharist. This is why I have spent so much time in this book examining issues that most books on worship-service planning overlook, such as the experiences that take place before people ever set foot in the sanctuary. Remember, people will remember how you made them feel.

PEOPLE TALKING ABOUT THEIR FORETASTE OF HEAVEN

The most beneficial result to come from the complete worship service is that people will talk about their foretaste of heaven. People throughout our culture are looking for another

163

world; they just do not know where it is, or what it is called, or how to get there. We, the people of God, need to give them the road map. Today, almost everyone is "spiritual," which can work to our advantage if we are willing to build new friendships. One of the most effective ways we do this is by coming away from our weekend services saying to ourselves, "We need to help someone else have this experience. We need to invite a family member or a friend to this wonderful foretaste of heaven."

Ultimately, nothing on this earth will bring people satisfaction. They will search like Solomon to satisfy the longing in their hearts with every pleasure imaginable but will ultimately find themselves disappointed. The only thing that will bring happiness is to be in God's place, with God's people, under God's rule, experiencing God's blessing.

People Are Looking for Hope

It is my prayer that as you set out on a journey to enhance your worship services, you will offer life to people. People are not just looking to be entertained. They are looking for life. They are looking for hope. They are looking for Jesus. They are looking for a foretaste of heaven. Do everything you can to ensure that they hear this message. Go out of your way to make the necessary improvements. Go out of your way to prepare the way for the Lord. Clear the obstacles, like the quality issues mentioned in this book, that get in the way of people hearing the Good News. When you are laser focused on this intent, you will provide the complete worship service for a community that is looking for heaven. May God richly bless you as you offer this precious gift, the complete worship service, to your community this weekend!

NOTES

Chapter 1: Longing for Heaven

1. Eric Hoffer, quoted on "Born to Motivate," www.borntomotivate.com/Happiness.html.

2. *Lost in Translation*, directed by Sofia Coppola (Universal Studios, 2003).

3. Calvin Miller, *The Finale* (Downers Grove, IL: InterVarsity Press, 1979), 21.

4. Quoted in Stephen Covey, *The Portable 7 Habits: Renewal, Nourishing Body, Mind, Heart, and Soul* (Salt Lake City: Franklin Covey, 1999), 10.

5. John Ortberg, *Dangers, Toils, and Snares: Resisting the Hidden Temptations of Ministry* (Portland: Multnomah, 1994), 99–100.

6. I first heard Rick Warren use this slogan at a Purpose-Driven Church conference.

7. Scott J. Hafemann, *The God of Promise and the Life of Faith* (Wheaton: Crossway, 2001), 36–37.

Chapter 2: Heaven

1. John Ortberg, "Our Secret Fears about Heaven," *Today's Christian Woman*, July/August 2003, 38–41.

Chapter 3: A Taste of Heaven, the Worship Service

1. I'm indebted to James Stewart for these thoughts. *Heralds of God* (Grand Rapids: Baker, 1972), 16.

2. Stanley Hauerwas and William H. Willimon, *Resident Aliens: Life in the Christian Colony* (Nashville: Abingdon, 1989), 52.

Chapter 4: Quality Matters

1. Stan Toler and Alan Nelson, *The Five Star Church* (Ventura, CA: Regal, 1999), 21.

2. Kirk Byron Jones, *The Jazz of Preaching: How to Preach with Great Freedom and Joy* (Nashville: Abingdon, 2004), 86.

3. Leith Anderson, *Leadership That Works: Hope and Direction for Church and Parachurch Leaders in Today's Complex World* (Minneapolis: Bethany, 1999), 113–14.

4. Quoted in Albert M. Wells Jr., *Inspiring Quotations Contemporary and Classic* (Nashville: Thomas Nelson, 1988), 160.

5. George Bernard Shaw, *Man and Superman*, 1903, act 3.

6. Jim Cymbala, *Fresh Wind, Fresh Fire* (Grand Rapids: Zondervan, 1997), 58–59.

7. Quoted in Toler and Nelson, *The Five Star Church*, 50.

Chapter 5: You've Gotta Be There

1. I first heard this slogan from Larry Osborn, senior pastor at Northcoast Church.

2. Wooddale Church, www.wooddale.org/faith_stories/default.

3. I'm indebted to Dann Spader for these ideas. For practical disciple-making tools, visit www.sonlife.com.

4. I first heard the term *scarcity mentality* from Tim Sanders at the 2004 Willow Creek Association Leadership Summit.

Chapter 7: Parking, Outside Signage, and Attendants

1. John Ortberg, *Leadership*, vol. 12. no. 3. Quoted on PreachingToday.com, http://www.preachingtoday.com/index.taf?_UserReference=BD2366EEA092 E94C42363E90&_function=illustration&_op=show_pf&IID=1991&sr=1.

Chapter 8: Developing Dynamic Guest Care Teams and Systems

1. Robert Spector and Patrick D. McCarthy, *The Nordstom Way* (New York: John Wiley & Sons, 1995), 125.

2. Quoted in Covey, *The Portable Seven Habits*, 30.

3. George Barna, *User Friendly Churches* (Ventura, CA: Regal, 1991), 177.

4. Cited by "Eutychus and His Kin," *Christianity Today*, June 3, 1977. Quoted on PreachingToday.com, http://www.preachingtoday.com/index.taf?_ UserReference=BD2366EEA092E94C42363E90&_function=illustration&_ op=show_pf&IID=3512&sr=1.

5. Michael D. Eisner, *Be Our Guest: Perfecting the Art of Customer Service* (New York: Disney Editions, 2001), 87.

6. John M. Shanahan, *The Most Brilliant Thoughts of All Time* (New York: Cliff Street Books, 1999), 3.

7. PreachingToday.com, http://www.preachingtoday.com/index.taf?_User Reference=61AE1F059E99613B421CC8D9&_function=illustration&_ op=show_pf&IID=13939&sr=1, illustration submitted by Greg Asimakoupoulos.

8. Eugene A. Maddox, Palatka, Florida. Quoted on PreachingToday.com, http://www.preachingtoday.com/index.taf?_UserReference=BD2366EEA092 E94C42363E90&_function=illustration&_op=show_pf& IID=13650&sr=1.

Chapter 9: The Worship Center

1. John Eldredge and Brent Curtis, *The Sacred Romance: Drawing Closer to the Heart of God* (Nashville: Thomas Nelson, 1997), 200–201.

Chapter 10: Music and the Arts

1. Ezra Pound, *ABC of Reading* (New York: New Directions Paperbook, 1934), 13.

2. I'm indebted to Darrell Johnson, my preaching professor at Fuller Seminary, for this slogan.

3. Quoted in Covey, *The Portable 7 Habits*, 43.

4. William D. Romanowski, *Eyes Wide Open: Looking for God in Popular Culture* (Grand Rapids: Brazos, 2001), 88.

Chapter 11: The Word of God

1. I'm indebted to Rick Warren for these ideas.

2. Bryan Chapell, *Christ-Centered Preaching: Redeeming the Expository Sermon* (Grand Rapids: Baker, 1994), 51.

3. David Buttrick, *Homiletic: Moves and Structures* (Philadelphia: Fortress, 1987), 5–6.

4. A special thanks to Darrell Johnson, who taught me these lessons while I was a student at Fuller Seminary.

5. James Stewart, *Heralds of God* (Grand Rapids: Baker, 1972), 13.

6. Chapell, *Christ-Centered Preaching*, 268.

7. Stewart, *Heralds of God*, 15–16.

Chapter 13: Thanksgiving as the Consummation of Joy

1. C. S. Lewis, *Reflections on the Psalms* (Orlando: Harcourt Brace Jovanovich, 1958), 95.

2. Ibid., 94.

BIBLIOGRAPHY

Anderson, Leith. *Leadership That Works: Hope and Direction for Church and Parachurch Leaders in Today's Complex World.* Minneapolis: Bethany House, 1999.

Barna, George. *User Friendly Churches: What Christians Need to Know about the Churches People Love to Go To.* Ventura, CA: Regal, 1991.

Beach, Nancy. *An Hour on Sunday: Creating Moments of Transformation and Wonder.* Grand Rapids: Zondervan, 2004.

Buttrick, David. *Homiletic: Moves and Structures.* Philadelphia: Fortress, 1987.

Chapell, Bryan. *Christ-Centered Preaching: Redeeming the Expository Sermon.* Grand Rapids: Baker, 1994.

Collins, Jim. *Good to Great.* New York: HarperCollins, 2001.

Curtis, Brent, and John Eldredge. *The Sacred Romance: Drawing Closer to the Heart of God.* Nashville: Thomas Nelson, 1997.

Cymbala, Jim. *Fresh Wind, Fresh Fire.* Grand Rapids: Zondervan, 1997.

Eisner, Michael D. *Be Our Guest: Perfecting the Art of Customer Service.* New York: Disney Editions, 2001.

Fraser, Peter, and Vernon Edwin Neal. *Reviewing the Movies: A Christian Response to Contemporary Film.* Wheaton: Crossway, 2000.

Hafemann, Scott J. *The God of Promise and the Life of Faith.* Wheaton: Crossway, 2001.

Hauerwas, Stanley, and William H. Willimon. *Resident Aliens: Life in the Christian Colony.* Nashville: Abingdon, 1989.

Jones, Kirk Byron. *The Jazz of Preaching: How to Preach with Great Freedom and Joy.* Nashville: Abingdon, 2004.

Keifert, Patrick R. *Welcoming the Stranger: A Public Theology of Worship and Evangelism.* Minneapolis: Fortress, 1992.

Lewis, C. S. *Reflections on the Psalms.* Orlando: Harcourt Brace Jovanovich, 1958.

Miller, Mark. *Experiential Storytelling: Rediscovering Narrative to Communicate God's Message.* El Cajon, CA: Zondervan, 2003.

Navarro, Kevin J. *The Complete Worship Leader.* Grand Rapids: Baker, 2001.

Romanowski, William D. *Eyes Wide Open: Looking for God in Popular Culture.* Grand Rapids: Brazos, 2001.

Saliers, Don E. *Worship Come to Its Senses.* Nashville: Abingdon, 1996.

Schaller, Lyle E. *44 Ways to Increase Church Attendance.* Nashville: Abingdon, 1988.

Spector, Robert, and Patrick D. McCarthy. *The Nordstrom Way: The Inside Story of America's #1 Customer Service Company.* New York: John Wiley & Sons, 1995.

Stewart, James. *Heralds of God.* Grand Rapids: Baker, 1972.

Toler, Stan, and Alan Nelson. *The Five Star Church.* Ventura, CA: Regal, 1999.

Warren, Rick. *The Purpose-Driven Church: Growing without Compromising Your Message and Mission.* Grand Rapids: Zondervan, 1995.

Kevin J. Navarro is the author of *The Complete Worship Leader* (Baker Books, 2001) and the senior pastor of Bethany Evangelical Free Church in Littleton, Colorado. He has been leading worship in the local church and with parachurch ministries for over twenty-two years. Navarro lives with his wife and five children in Centennial, Colorado.

Navarro attended the University of Northern Colorado, where he received his Bachelor of Music and Bachelor of Music Education. He also graduated from Denver Seminary with a Master of Divinity and from Fuller Theological Seminary with a Doctorate of Ministry. This blend of musical and theological education allows him to teach about worship as an artist, theologian, and pastor. His mission is celebrating the work of Christ through creative communication.

Navarro was also an international director for the Continental Singers. He led the Continentals through five continents. He has also been a guest speaker at national conferences and Bible conferences around the world. This international experience is reflected in Navarro's teaching as it pertains to understanding styles of worship, art forms, and cultural dynamics in the local church.

For information about speaking engagements related to *The Complete Worship Leader* or *The Complete Worship Service*, contact Kevin J. Navarro at kevinjnavarro@hotmail.com.

Especially for Worship Leaders
from Kevin J. Navarro

How do you draw people into God's presence?

This book explains the four elements that are crucial to becoming an effective worship leader: theology, discipleship, artistry, and leadership. You'll also find insights into building a worship team, engaging the five senses in worship, using new technology, and more!

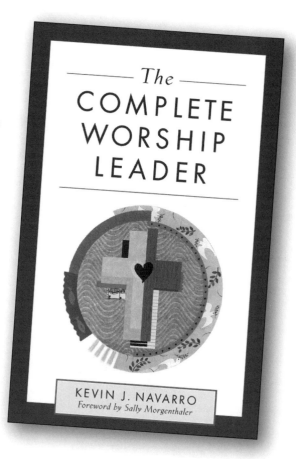

"Fellow worship leaders ... God calls us to a supreme walk of faith and intentionality. May this much-needed book serve as your ready guide for a most exciting journey."

—Sally Morganthaler, author of *Worship Evangelism*

"The term 'worship leader' describes a new way of conceiving of worship ministry leadership. Kevin's book explores this new approach in a helpful way by pointing to the foundational issues at stake for anyone in a worship role—as a volunteer, or part-time or full-time staff."

—Robb Redman, contributing editor, *Worship Leader*